# WORLD HISTORY SERIES ■ ■ ■

# The American Revolution

## Titles in the World History Series

**_HISTORY SERIES_** ■ ■ ■

# The American Revolution

by
**Bonnie L. Lukes**

Lucent Books, P.O. Box 289011, San Diego, CA 92198-9011

Library of Congress Cataloging-in-Publication Data

Lukes, Bonnie L.
    The American Revolution / by Bonnie L. Lukes.
        p.  cm.—(World history series)
    Includes bibliographical references and index.
    Summary: Focuses on events precipitating the Revolution,
as well as events during and just after it.
    ISBN 1-56006-287-8
    1. United States—History—Revolution, 1775–1783—
Juvenile literature.    [1. United States—History—Revolution,
1775–1783.]    I. Title.    II. Series.
E208.L97    1996
973.3—dc20                                                      95–50721
                                                                   CIP
                                                                    AC

Copyright 1996 by Lucent Books, Inc., P.O. Box 289011,
San Diego, California 92198-9011

Printed in the U.S.A.

# Contents

# Foreword

Each year on the first day of school, nearly every history teacher faces the task of explaining why his or her students should study history. One logical answer to this question is that exploring what happened in our past explains how the things we often take for granted—our customs, ideas, and institutions—came to be. As statesman and historian Winston Churchill put it, "Every nation or group of nations has its own tale to tell. Knowledge of the trials and struggles is necessary to all who would comprehend the problems, perils, challenges, and opportunities which confront us today." Thus, a study of history puts modern ideas and institutions in perspective. For example, though the founders of the United States were talented and creative thinkers, they clearly did not invent the concept of democracy. Instead, they adapted some democratic ideas that had originated in ancient Greece and with which the Romans, the British, and others had experimented. An exploration of these cultures, then, reveals their very real connection to us through institutions that continue to shape our daily lives.

Another reason often given for studying history is the idea that lessons exist in the past from which contemporary societies can benefit and learn. This idea, although controversial, has always been an intriguing one for historians. Those that agree that society can benefit from the past often quote philosopher George Santayana's famous statement, "Those who cannot remember the past are condemned to repeat it." Historians who ascribe to Santayana's philosophy believe that, for example, studying the events that led up to the major world wars or other significant historical events would allow society to chart a different and more favorable course in the future.

Just as difficult as convincing students to realize the importance of studying history is the search for useful and interesting supplementary materials that present historical events in a context that can be easily understood. The volumes in Lucent Books' World History Series attempt to present a broad, balanced, and penetrating view of the march of history. Ancient Egypt's important wars and rulers, for example, are presented against the rich and colorful backdrop of Egyptian religious, social, and cultural developments. The series engages the reader by enhancing historical events with these cultural contexts. For example, in *Ancient Greece*, the text covers the role of women in that society. Slavery is discussed in *The Roman Empire*, as well as how slaves earned their freedom. The numerous and varied aspects of everyday life in these and other societies are explored in each volume of the series. Additionally, the series covers the major political, cultural, and philosophical ideas as the torch of civilization is passed from ancient Mesopotamia and Egypt, through Greece, Rome, Medieval Europe, and other world cultures, to the modern day.

The material in the series is formatted in a thorough, precise, and organized manner. Each volume offers the reader a comprehensive and clearly written overview of an important historical event or period. The topic under discussion is placed in a broad historical context. For example, *The Italian Renaissance* begins with a discussion of the High Middle Ages and the loss of central control that allowed certain Italian cities to develop artistically. The book ends by looking forward to the Reformation and interpreting the societal changes that grew out of the Renaissance. Thus, students are not only involved in an historical era, but also enveloped by the events leading up to that era and the events following it.

One important and unique feature in the World History Series is the primary and secondary source quotations that richly supplement each volume. These quotes are useful in a number of ways. First, they allow students access to sources they would not normally be exposed to because of the difficulty and obscurity of the original source. The quotations range from interesting anecdotes to farsighted cultural perspectives and are drawn from historical witnesses both past and present. Second, the quotes demonstrate how and where historians themselves derive their information on the past as they strive to reach a consensus on historical events. Lastly, all of the quotes are footnoted, familiarizing students with the citation process and allowing them to verify quotes and/or look up the original source if the quote piques their interest.

Finally, the books in the World History Series provide a detailed launching point for further research. Each book contains a bibliography specifically geared toward student research. A second, annotated bibliography introduces students to all the sources the author consulted when compiling the book. A chronology of important dates gives students an overview, at a glance, of the topic covered. Where applicable, a glossary of terms is included.

In short, the series is designed not only to acquaint readers with the basics of history, but also to make them aware that their lives are a part of an ongoing human saga. Perhaps they will then come to the same realization as famed historian Arnold Toynbee. In his monumental work, *A Study of History*, he wrote about becoming aware of history flowing through him in a mighty current, and of his own life "welling like a wave in the flow of this vast tide."

# Important Dates in the History of the American Revolution

1607 1620 1630 1660 1688 1756 1763 1764 1765 1766 1767 1768 1770 1772 1773

**1607**
Virginia Company establishes a settlement at Jamestown

**1620**
Pilgrims establish colony at Plymouth

**1630**
Puritans migrate to New England

**1660**
First of the British Navigation Acts is enacted

**1688**
Glorious Revolution

**1756**
French and Indian War begins

**1763**
Treaty of Paris ends French and Indian War

**1764**
Sugar Act is passed

**1765**
Stamp Act is passed; Virginia Resolves are passed; Rockingham replaces Grenville as prime minister; Stamp Act Congress

**1766**
Stamp Act is repealed; Declaratory Act is passed; Pitt replaces Rockingham as prime minister

**1767**
First Townshend Act is passed; customs officials arrive in Boston

**1768**
Massachusetts circular letter is written; riot over seizure of Hancock's sloop *Liberty*; delegates from all over Massachusetts meet to consider using force against the British; British troops arrive in Boston

**1770**
Lord North becomes prime minister; Boston Massacre; Townshend duties repealed except on tea

**1772**
*Gaspee* burned; Boston Committee of Correspondence is formed

**1773**
Virginia calls for intercolonial Committees of Correspondence; Tea Act is passed; Boston Tea Party

**1774**
Intolerable Acts are passed; First Continental Congress meets; Continental Association is formed

1774  1775  1776  1777  1778  1779  1780  1781  1782  1783  1786  1787  1788  1789

**1775**
Battles of Lexington and Concord; Second Continental Congress meets; Battle of Bunker Hill; Olive Branch Petition is submitted to England; George III proclaims Americans in open rebellion

**1776**
Thomas Paine publishes *Common Sense*; British troops evacuate Boston; Declaration of Independence; British occupy New York City; Washington's victory at Trenton

**1777**
British occupy Philadelphia; Continental Army winters at Valley Forge; British are defeated at Saratoga

**1778**
France enters the war

**1779**
Spain enters the war

**1780**
Charleston, South Carolina, falls to British; Battle of Camden

**1781**
Articles of Confederation ratified; American and French forces defeat British at Yorktown

**1782**
Treaty of Paris is signed

**1783**
Treaty of Paris is ratified, ending war

**1786**
Annapolis Convention

**1787**
Shays's Rebellion; Constitutional Convention; first of the *Federalist* papers is published

**1788**
Constitution is ratified by New Hampshire, the ninth state to accept it, and is declared to be law by Congress

**1789**
George Washington is inaugurated as first president; Bill of Rights is passed by Congress

# Inheritance of Liberty

The American Revolution began officially on July 4, 1776, with the signing of the Declaration of Independence. But its seeds—in the form of a written charter from the king of England—had arrived with the English settlers in Jamestown in 1607. The charter guaranteed the settlers all the "priviledges, immunities and franchises [freedoms], that have at any time been held, enjoyed, and possessed, by the people of Great Britain."[1] Colonists cherished those rights, and their descendants eventually risked everything to protect them. In a sense, that charter was America's first constitution.

As historian Bernard Bailyn has noted:

> The colonists' attitude to the whole world of politics and government was fundamentally shaped by the root assumption that they, as Britishers, shared in a unique inheritance of liberty.[2]

Yet by 1763 many colonial Americans began to fear the loss of that legacy. They had fought alongside Britain during the French and Indian War. Their efforts forced the French to give up their large colonial holdings in North America. After the war Britain moved a standing army of royal troops into the colonies to prevent a French return to North America. Parlia-

ment felt the colonies should help pay for maintaining the army and passed laws to raise money for that purpose. The money was to come from duties, or taxes, placed on colonial trade.

The colonists considered such taxes to be improper because no one from North America had a seat in Parliament, the British legislature, which had voted for the taxes. The colonists summarized their position with the slogan "No taxation without representation," for they believed that only their assemblies, made up of persons they elected, had the right to tax them. They also feared that the British government would end up depriving the colonists of all control of their internal affairs. The passage of the Stamp Act in 1765, which imposed yet another tax, confirmed these fears. If Parliament was allowed to enforce the Stamp Act, who knew what the faraway lawmakers would demand next.

## Reluctant Revolutionaries

The colonists could see no way to preserve their rights except to resist the laws, even if it meant war with their beloved mother country. However, they were reluctant to consider themselves revolutionaries—even

*(Above) The Battle of Lexington. American colonists felt they had no choice but to resist Britain's efforts to control and subjugate them. (Below) Jefferson drafts the Declaration of Independence, the document that gave voice to American colonists' desires to establish their own independent nation.*

at the moment of declaring independence. Thomas Jefferson, in his first draft of the Declaration of Independence, demonstrated in one wistful, poignant line how devastating it was for the colonists to break away from England. He wrote, "We might have been a free and a great people together."[3]

However, such a union was not to be. Instead, in 1776, thirteen colonies declared their independence and began the process of becoming a nation. They had begun with fewer than three hundred immigrants in an isolated wilderness. They survived to become, as Thomas Jefferson phrased it, "the last great hope of the world."[4] How this was accomplished is the story of the American Revolution.

# 1 Old World to New World

On June 7, 1776, Richard Henry Lee of Virginia placed a resolution before the Continental Congress declaring that "These United Colonies are, and of right ought to be, free and independent states."[5] The resolution was adopted, and on July 4 the colonies declared their independence from England. Lee, along with Sam Adams, John Hancock, and other Patriot leaders, was now a rebel in danger of being hanged for treason.

Yet, only a decade earlier the colonists had boasted of belonging to the British Empire, declaring the British constitution to be "the most free one, and by far the best, now existing on earth."[6] What had changed? To understand, it is necessary to begin with the English settlers who migrated to the New World in the seventeenth century.

## English Colonization in North America

Britain's thirteen colonies in North America were not founded by either the king or Parliament. They were founded by trading companies seeking a profit, by reformers searching for a place to carry out their dreams of a perfect society, and by religious groups seeking freedom to worship as they pleased.

Jamestown, the first permanent English settlement in North America, was financed by the Virginia Company of London—a group of investors who sold shares of stock in their company and used the capital to finance overseas explorations. The company secured a charter from King James I that guaranteed "all the rights of Englishmen" to the colonists and their descendants. That set an important precedent for future colonies. With the exception of New Jersey and Delaware, all the colonies would have such a charter. These charters formed the foundation of American rights and liberties.

## "All Things to Do"

When the Jamestown settlers arrived in North America in 1607, they had more to do than just build homes and farms. The colonists, as one of them wrote, had "all things to do, as in the beginning of the world."[7] They needed to establish a community—complete with churches and schools—where families could grow and thrive. Economic success depended on finding a profitable product to export.

As it happened, however, the first group of Jamestown settlers consisted, for the most part, of soft-handed gentlemen adventurers not accustomed to working. They expected to find gold lying on the ground for them to harvest and take back to England. Instead they found hordes of malaria-carrying mosquitoes. The food they purchased from friendly Native Americans made them ill, and their hastily constructed huts let in the rain and cold. Still they wasted valuable time searching for gold when they should have been planting corn and taking advantage of the abundance of fish and game. They fought among themselves and refused to work. Within three months of their arrival, starvation and illness had taken their toll. Only 38 of the original 144 settlers remained alive.

Captain John Smith, who emerged as the strongest leader, begged the Virginia Company to send him "but thirty carpenters, husbandmen [farmers], gardeners, fishermen, and blacksmiths" rather than "a thousand such gallants [fashionable gentlemen] as were sent to me, that would do nothing but complain, curse and despair."[8]

*Captain John Smith tried to lead the English settlers in Jamestown through the disaster of their first year.*

## Free Land Offered to New Settlers

By 1609 the Virginia Company realized that Jamestown needed ordinary farmers who could grow the food necessary to sustain the colony. To attract this kind of settler, the company promised emigrants free land at the end of seven years' labor. Nine years later, that offer was improved: The company promised fifty acres of land out-right to those who could pay their own fare across the ocean to Virginia:

> Whosoever transports himselfe or any other at his owne charge unto Virginia shall for each person so transported before Midsummer 1625 have to him and his heires for ever fiftie Acres of Land.[9]

This was a significant event because it established individual landownership in the colonies. Land became a powerful magnet that attracted people to North America. These settlers, unlike the first Jamestown adventurers, were firmly committed to the New World. They did not come expecting to make a quick profit and leave. The opportunity to own land

*English settlers braved the ocean to come to the New World in hopes of attaining land—and the economic and political independence it granted.*

gave them a stake in America. They came determined to stay and make new lives for themselves and their children.

But owning property meant much more than economic independence to these immigrants. It meant they could have a say in how they were governed, because property owners could vote. Whereas in England only a small percentage of men could vote because property ownership was limited to the privileged few, in the colonies, most men could vote because most men owned property. Every colony that participated in the Revolution had a representative assembly of men who had been elected by property holders. In America as in England, women could neither run for office nor vote in elections.

## Origin of Self-Government in America

From the time the English settlers first landed in Jamestown, they sought representative government. The Virginia Com-

pany had been chartered and empowered by the Crown (that is, the monarch) to appoint governors and officers to govern the colony of Virginia. In 1619—struggling to make the colony profitable and pressured by leading settlers for a voice in local government—the company directed the colonists to assemble a representative group of settlers. This assembly was called the House of Burgesses. Although meant to act only as a periodic adviser, the House of Burgesses slowly grew into a legitimate governing body. It even survived after the Virginia Company went bankrupt in 1624.

At that time the monarch, King James, canceled the company's charter and established a royal government in Virginia. But the House of Burgesses, after a brief suspension, continued as a part of the government that made laws along with the royal governor and his council. Historian Darrett B. Rutman writes about this in *The Morning of America*:

In such an off-handed way did the beginnings of self-government come to the colonies: the monarch granting self-regulation to private persons backing colonies and the private persons, finding it necessary to make colonization by Englishmen successful, sharing their powers of self-regulation with the settlers.[10]

By the end of the seventeenth century, every colony had an elected assembly. Colonies were divided into townships, each of which sent elected representatives to the assembly. Unlike members of the House of Commons in England, the assembly delegates were required to be resi-dents of the area they represented. By 1763 the assemblies had established their right to pass laws and levy taxes within the colonies. The growing power of the assemblies was a major factor among the forces that led to revolution.

## The Colonies in a Mercantile World

In the seventeenth century, Britain—intent on gaining a foothold in North Amer-

---

### Wilderness Experience

*William Bradford was the second governor of the tiny colony of Plymouth settled in 1620. In his history, "Of Plimoth Plantation," reprinted in* U.S. Colonial History, Readings and Documents, *edited by David Hawke, he described the dangers the Plymouth Pilgrims encountered in the New World.*

"Being thus arrived in a good harbor and brought safe to land, they fell upon their knees and blessed the God of heaven, who had brought them over the vast and furious ocean and delivered them from all the perils and miseries thereof. . . . Being thus passed the vast ocean, and a sea of troubles before . . . their [departure], . . . they had now no friends to welcome them nor inns to entertain or refresh their weatherbeaten bodies; no houses or much less towns to repair to, to seek for succor [aid]. And . . . it was winter. . . . Besides what could they see but a hideous and desolate wilderness, full of wild beasts and wild men—and what multitudes there might be of them they knew not. . . . If they looked behind them, there was the mighty ocean [over] which they had passed and was now a . . . gulf to separate them from all the civil parts of the world. . . . What could now sustain them but the spirit of God and his Grace? Ought not the children of these fathers rightly say: 'Our fathers were Englishmen which came over this great ocean and were ready to perish in this wilderness but they cried unto the Lord, and He heard their voice.'"

ica—could not have imagined a time when her colonies would rebel. After all, trade was England's major motive for establishing its transatlantic colonies. Moreover, the British economy was dominated by the theory of mercantilism, which held, among other things, that colonies existed only for the benefit of the mother country. In practice, this meant that the colonies were to supply raw materials, which workers and craftspeople in Britain would transform into finished products. Finally, the manufactured goods would be sold back to the colonies. Both the colonies and England would thus have a protected market and each would prosper.

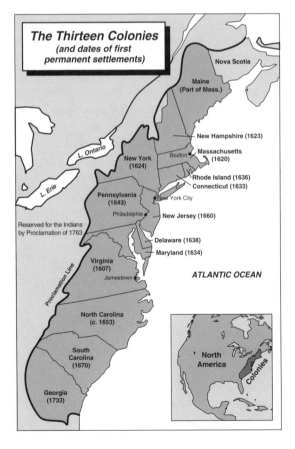

The Thirteen Colonies
(and dates of first permanent settlements)

Nova Scotia

Maine
(Part of Mass.)

L. Ontario

New Hampshire (1623)

New York
(1624)

Boston

Massachusetts
(1620)

L. Erie

Rhode Island (1636)
Connecticut (1633)

Pennsylvania
(1643)

New York City

Philadelphia

New Jersey (1660)

Reserved for the Indians
by Proclamation of 1763

Delaware (1638)

Maryland (1634)

Virginia
(1607)

Jamestown

ATLANTIC OCEAN

Proclamation Line

North Carolina
(c. 1653)

South
Carolina
(1670)

North
America

Colonies

Georgia
(1733)

## The Navigation Acts

In the early years, England saw little need for any formal regulation of colonial trade outside of passing a law that forbade tobacco growers to export their product anywhere but to England. However, by 1651 the colonists were trading profitably with the Dutch. The mother country did not approve of this practice. Consequently, in 1660, to stop the colonies from trading with other countries, Parliament passed the first of the Navigation Acts. This act permitted only English or colonial ships that were manned by English or colonial sailors to bring goods into England, Ireland, and the colonies. Later acts specified colonial products that could be exported only to England and imposed a tax on some imports into the colonies. The Navigation Acts also tried to prevent the colonists from competing with established industries in the mother country. For example, laws forbidding the colonists from importing knitting frames were meant to keep Americans from competing with the English textile industry.

The colonists did not oppose the Navigation Acts, because mercantilism provided a stable market for their goods. In any event, the acts could not be enforced. Evasion was easy because England was far away, and it was easy to bribe underpaid customs officers—generally friends and neighbors of colonial producers. Smuggling, too, became an accepted profession in the colonies. Even John Hancock, one of the signers of the Declaration of Independence, was suspected of having made his fortune through smuggling. Reports of these activities, often exaggerated, planted early seeds of suspicion and distrust between the colonies and the mother country. However, most colonials were content to outwardly accept the relatively mild restrictions of the Navigation Acts. They enjoyed being a part of the British Empire, and the colonies were a long way from being a united country.

## Common Threads

As the thirteen colonies matured, each developed a distinct personality along with an overabundance of regional pride. Colonists often took verbal potshots at one another, as New Englander John Adams did in this comment regarding New Yorkers:

> With all the opulence and splendor of this city, there is little good breeding to be found. . . . At their entertainment, there is no conversation that is agreeable; there is no modesty, no attention to one another. They talk very loud, very fast and altogether.[11]

But despite the regional differences that developed, the colonists shared a common history. Mostly of English descent, they took great pride in their heritage. In religion, they were overwhelmingly Protestant. And although four or five large cities existed, most of the colonists were farmers. Also, because so many owned land, the differences between the rich and the poor were not as extreme as they continued to be in Europe. There were, of course, always some who were better off than others, but as a traveler in the colonies in 1772 noted:

> The poorest laborer on the shore of the Delaware thinks himself entitled to

deliver his sentiments in matters of religion or politics with as much freedom as the gentleman or scholar. Indeed there is less distinction among the citizens of Philadelphia, than among those of any civilized city in the world. Riches give none. For every man expects one day or another to be upon a footing with his wealthiest neighbor.[12]

The African slaves, who shared few of the benefits of America, were the exception.

Another strong link between the colonists was the experience of surviving the hardships of the wilderness. With the mother country an ocean away—at least a six-week voyage—they had been forced to rely on their own skill and ingenuity. They had battled disease and scrounged for food to feed their families. And they had been forced to invent, as they went along, whatever kind of local government best served their needs. But those difficult times toughened and strengthened the colonists, creating what Hector St. John de Crèvecoeur, a French immigrant, called "this new man." Thus the colonists emerged with a self-assurance that was not always understood or appreciated in the mother country.

## England's Legacy of Liberty

Despite this growing self-reliance, the colonists revered England's constitution and took great pride in belonging to the British Empire. The strength of the English government lay in the balance of power between the Crown and the two houses of Parliament: the House of Lords

*The crown of England is offered to William and Mary in the bloodless coup that became known as the Glorious Revolution. Britain had a strong history of democracy, a legacy New World settlers wanted to emulate.*

and the House of Commons. The House of Lords consisted of members of the nobility and bishops of the Church of England. The House of Commons was made up of representatives elected by property-owning subjects.

During the sixteenth and seventeenth centuries, the Crown had enormous power in England. In 1685 King James II ascended to the throne. A Roman Catholic, he was unpopular with the majority of his subjects, who were Protestant. And he was feared because of his insistence on the absolute power of the Crown. He began appointing Roman Catholics to high government posts, and when Parliament resisted, he arrogantly dismissed the entire body.

This could not be tolerated, and a group of prominent Protestant leaders—fearing a Catholic conspiracy—secretly plotted his downfall. In 1688 they invited William of Orange, king of the Netherlands, to invade England and take over the throne with his wife Mary, James's Protestant daughter. James decided to abdicate [give up the throne] rather than fight. His abdication is known as the Glorious Revolution, because there was little bloodshed.

## Fruits of the Glorious Revolution

The Glorious Revolution ended forever (in England) the notion that kings ruled by God-given, or divine, right. The authority of the Crown was greatly reduced, and

Parliament became the predominant power. It was a victory for the English people because it produced a Declaration of Rights. This document—much of which would serve as a pattern for the American Bill of Rights—reaffirmed such rights as freedom of speech and the right to trial by a jury. It further guaranteed that no British subjects could be taxed without their consent, given through their elected representatives in the House of Commons.

The Glorious Revolution affected the colonists in two ways. It caused political upheavals in New England, New York, and Maryland, where all colonial officials loyal to James were forced out of power. But the most powerful and long-lasting effect was ideological. The British colonists in America, as they watched the drama in England unfold, learned a lesson they wouldn't forget—"that the rights and liberties of a free people have to be fought for and that in the mother country such a struggle had been crowned with success."[13]

## Little Parliaments

By the mid-eighteenth century, the three branches of colonial government resembled roughly those in England. The royal

---

### The First Assembly

*The first meeting of the House of Burgesses in Virginia took place on July 30, 1619. It was an awe-inspiring occasion for the colonial Americans to join His Majesty's council and governor.* U.S. Colonial History, Readings and Documents *contains the account of this momentous beginning of representative government in America.*

"The most convenient place we could find to sit in was the choir of the church. . . . Sir George Yeardley, the governor, being set down in his accustomed place [in the main part of the church and] those of the Council of Estate sat next him on both [sides] except only the secretary, [and] appointed speaker, who sat right before him; John Twine, clerk of the General Assembly, being placed next the speaker, and Thomas Pierse, the sergeant, standing at the bar to be ready for any service the assembly should command him. But . . . all the burgesses took their places in the choir till a prayer was said by Mr. Buck, the minister, that it would please God to guide us and sanctify all our proceedings to His own glory and the good of this plantation [colony]. Prayer being ended, . . . all the burgesses were [asked] to retire themselves into the body of the church, [and] they were called in order and by name, and so every man . . . took the oath of supremacy [renouncing the pope's powers in favor of those held by the monarch], and then entered the assembly."

---

governor, appointed in England, represented the king. The council, appointed by the governor, was similar to the House of Lords. And the elected assemblies paralleled the House of Commons. In fact, the colonials increasingly considered their assemblies to be "little parliaments," entitled to supreme legislative power over colonial domestic matters. England, however, regarded the colonial assemblies as mere imitations of Parliament, existing only because the mother country permitted them to do so.

Despite the similar structures of English and colonial governments, important ideological differences had developed, particularly in the area of representation. England considered all the people in her empire to be *virtually,* or indirectly, represented. However, in the colonies—as a result of the popularly elected assemblies to which each county elected its own representatives—the concept of absolute or direct representation had evolved. This had not been a problem during the long period known as "salutary neglect" when the British government avoided interfering in colonial affairs in order to allow the colonies to develop naturally. England had been too busy with European conflicts to recognize the growing power of the colonial assemblies. Consequently, in 1764, when Parliament taxed the colonists to help pay off the empire's war debts, England was unprepared for the colonists' outraged reaction.

The colonists held to their position— "No taxation without representation"— but the British insisted that the colonies *were* represented in Parliament through virtual representation. James Otis, one of the earliest leaders of the Patriot cause, disagreed. You could, he wrote, "as well prove that the British House of Commons . . . represent all the people of the globe as [to say it represents] those in America."[14] This question of representation led to a struggle for power between the colonial assemblies and Parliament that would culminate in the American Revolution.

## A New Breed

In addition to differences over representation, the mother country and the colonists had grown apart in other ways. The second and third generations of colonists— those born in America and growing up in the wilderness—did not share with their parents and grandparents an identification with England. Most of them had never been there, and they experienced little contact with English officials because England—involved in almost constant warfare—had allowed the colonies to go their own way. Out of touch with the political standards of the Old World, the colonists established their own. They developed political practices that, while they were English, bore the distinct imprint of colonial America. And in the mid-1760s, when they felt their liberty threatened by acts of imperial power, this new generation of colonists rebelled. They were not intimidated by the mighty British Empire.

## Hail Britannia

As might be expected, the self-sufficient colonial Americans believed in the right to control their local affairs. After the Glorious Revolution in the seventeenth century,

# Song of the Early Colonists

*According to the Massachusetts Historical Collection, the first written record was made of this song in 1785 as it was recited by a ninety-six-year-old woman. It is a realistic description of colonial life in New England. These excerpts are taken from* The Annals of America.

Forefathers' Song

"New England's annoyances you that would know them,
Pray ponder these verses which briefly doth show them.
The place where we live is a wilderness wood,
Where grass is much wanting that's fruitful and good:
Being commonly covered with ice and with snow; . . .

But when the Spring opens we then take the hoe,
And make the ground ready to plant and to sow;
Our corn being planted and seed being sown,
The worms destroy much before it is grown; . . .

And now our garments begin to grow thin,
And wool is much wanted to card and to spin;
If we can get a garment to cover without,
Our other in-garments are clout [patches] upon clout. . . .

If fresh meat be [lacking] to fill up our dish,
We have carrots and turnips as much as we wish:
And if there's a mind for a delicate dish
We repair to the clam-banks, and there we catch fish.
Instead of pottage [hearty soup] and puddings and
        custards and pies,
Our pumpkins and parsnips are common supplies;
We have pumpkins at morning and pumpkins at noon,
If it was not for pumpkins we should be undone!
If barley be wanting to make into malt,
We must be contented, and think it no fault;
For we can make liquor to sweeten our lips,
Of pumpkins and parsnips and walnut-tree chips. . . .

But you whom the Lord intends hither to bring,
Forsake not the honey for fear of the sting;
But bring both a quiet and contented mind,
And all needful blessings you surely will find."

*British soldiers address Native Americans during the French and Indian War. The British victory during the war left American colonists proud to be Britons and satisfied with the mother country. England, on the other hand, was dismayed by the colonists' unruly independence.*

they continually agitated for more self-government. As a result, there had been friction between the colonial assemblies and the Crown, and between the assemblies and the royal governors in the colonies.

Nevertheless, by the end of the French and Indian War in 1763 the colonists were reasonably satisfied with the compromises between home rule and imperial rule. Much of the seven-year French and Indian War—a war undertaken by England to destroy French trade in North America—had been fought on American soil, and the colonists prided themselves on their part in the English victory. The colonists had fought alongside the British soldiers, suffering a high rate of casualties. Boston, a town of about two thousand families, lost seven hundred men. All their grievances against the mother country faded away. The colonists had no thoughts of separating from England and had never felt more patriotic. The British Empire ruled, and they were Britons.

The British, on the other hand, had gotten a firsthand look at their unruly colonies, and they were not happy with what they had seen.

# 2 Colonial America by 1763

When England and her thirteen colonies came face to face during the French and Indian War, illusions were shattered on both sides. Neither would ever see the other in quite the same way again.

The British were appalled that the colonists continued to trade at the enemy ports of the Spanish and French West Indies throughout the war. A further irritation was the colonial assemblies' reluctance to provide money and men for the war, even when England promised reimbursement. In fact, many assemblies took advantage of the situation, seeing in the British need for funds an opportunity to bargain for concessions from the royal governors.

## British Refuse to Acknowledge Militia Officers

The colonists complained about the arrogant behavior of the British troops and their demands for quarters and provisions. The British had also practiced impressment, or the forced enlistment of ablebodied male colonists in their navy and army. But what had most angered the Americans was England's contempt for the colonial militia.

Each colony maintained a group of armed volunteers known as a militia, to be

*An American soldier is impressed into the British Navy. Conflicts between the British and American militaries created divisions between the English and the colonists.*

## Freedom: A Natural Right of All People

*James Otis's popular* The Rights of the British Colonies Asserted and Proved, *published in 1764, was reprinted in England and in the colonies. In this excerpt from* Pamphlets of the American Revolution, 1750–1776, *edited by Bernard Bailyn, Otis condemns the practice of slavery.*

"The colonists are by the law of nature freeborn, as indeed all men are, white or black. . . . Does it follow that 'tis right to enslave a man because he is black? Will short curled hair like wool instead of Christian hair, as 'tis called by those whose hearts are as hard as the nether [lower] millstone, help the argument? Can any logical inference in favor of slavery be drawn from a flat nose, a long or a short face? Nothing . . . can be said in favor of a trade that is the most shocking violation of the law of nature, has a direct tendency to diminish the idea of the inestimable value of liberty, and makes every dealer in it a tyrant. . . . It is a clear truth that those who every day barter away other men's liberty will soon care little for their own.

'There is nothing more evident,' says [John] Locke, than 'that creatures of the same species and rank . . . born to the same advantages of nature and the use of the same faculties, should also be equal one among another without subordination and subjection. . . . The natural liberty of men is to be free from any superior power on earth, and not to be under the will or legislative authority of man, but only to have the law of nature for his rule.' "

called on in emergencies. British officers had little respect for the militiamen and refused to recognize any militia officer above the rank of captain. Thus colonial majors and colonels had to take orders from British officers lower in rank. This upset a young Virginian named George Washington, who was colonel of the Virginia Regiment. When Washington learned that his unit was to be reorganized into companies—with captain as the highest rank—he resigned from the army, preferring to serve as a volunteer rather than accept the demotion. Later in the war, the royal governor of Virginia reestablished the Virginia Regiment and Washington resumed his rank of colonel.

The British attitude toward the militia is apparent in the comments of General Lord Albermarle, the British ambassador to France:

*Washington & many Such,* may have courage & resolution, but they have no Knowledge or Experience in our Profession; consequently there can be no dependence on them! Officers, & good ones must be sent to Discipline the Militia, & to Lead them on.[15]

Although these grievances faded in the first flush of victory over the French, the colonists would not forget the humiliation. "And once independence was in the wind, [those] memories would lead men to think more favorably of a break than they might have done otherwise, and to consider a break feasible."[16]

In addition, despite heavy colonial casualties and difficulties with the British soldiers, the colonists emerged from the French and Indian War with increased confidence in their military abilities. At the beginning of that war, they had witnessed the British army losing battle after battle. They had watched demoralized British soldiers flee from the enemy. As a result, they no longer regarded the British military as invincible—a discovery that would take on added importance twelve years later. As historian Darrett Rutman writes:

Colonial militiamen watching the awesome advance of British redcoats on Breed's Hill in 1775 could comfort themselves with the thought that similar redcoats had been defeated on the Monongahela [River] and at [Fort] Ticonderoga [by the French and Indians].[17]

## England's Great Expectations

In 1763, the victory over the French established Great Britain as the predominant power in North America. And for the first time in a long while England was not at war with anyone. She turned her attention to the colonies, determined to bring her willful American children to heel. The colonies were to be reminded that they were a possession of the British Empire. And that as such, they were expected to be grateful, cooperative, and obedient. They were to supply money and men when told to do so, because that was the purpose of colonies.

But it would not be that simple. Many things had changed in the 150 years since Jamestown had been carved out of the wilderness. The colonists were now an expanding and maturing people who had developed ideas and ways that differed from those of their British cousins.

## Growing Population in the Colonies

One change in the colonies was the growing population. Doubling every generation, it had reached almost two million by the end of the French and Indian War. Large families accounted for some of the growth, but the colonies had also received large groups of immigrants. Not all these immigrants were English. Germans and Scots-Irish made up one-quarter of the population, and approximately one-eighth were those brought by force, the Africans. Although colonial society retained its English leadership and characteristics, immigrants would, in time, be absorbed, or assimilated, into the culture. Of the fifty-six signers of the Declaration of Independence, eighteen were non-English, and eight of those eighteen were born outside the colonies.

# Powhatan's Speech to Captain John Smith

*In 1609 Powhatan, a leader of the Algonquin tribe, delivered this speech to Captain John Smith, the leader of the Virginia colony. For the most part, Smith and Powhatan managed to coexist peacefully, but Powhatan's fears for his people proved to be prophetic. The speech is included in* 100 Key Documents in American Democracy, *edited by Peter B. Levy.*

*Chief Powhatan sought peaceful relations with the American colonists. Unfortunately, the conflict between Native American and white settler would end in tragedy.*

"I am now grown old, and must soon die, and the succession must descend, in order to my brothers . . . and then to my two sisters. . . . I wish their experience was equal to mine; and that your love to us might not be less than ours to you. Why should you take by force that from us which you can have by love? Why should you destroy us, who have provided you with food? What can you get by war? . . . What is the cause of your jealousy? You see us unarmed, and willing to supply your wants if you will come in a friendly manner, and not with swords and guns, as to invade an enemy. I am not so simple, as not to know it is better to eat good meat, . . . to sleep quietly with my women and children; to laugh and be merry with the English; and, being their friend to have copper, hatchets, and whatever else I want, than to [flee], to lie cold in the woods, feed upon acorns, . . . and to be so hunted, that I cannot rest, eat or sleep. In such circumstances, my men must watch, and if a twig should but break, all would cry out, *'Here comes Capt. Smith'*; and so, in this miserable manner . . . end my miserable life; and, Capt. Smith, this *might* be soon your fate too, through your rashness. . . . I, therefore, exhort you to peaceable councils; and above all, I insist that the guns and swords, the cause of all our jealousy and uneasiness, be removed and sent away."

# Colonial Social Structure

As the population grew, a class structure developed in the colonies. The early English settlers came to North America from a society of rigid class divisions. In the beginning, they tried to follow those Old World patterns. For example, the Puritans in Massachusetts could not sit anywhere they pleased in church. They were assigned pews according to age, parentage, social position, wealth, and occupation.

But like many cultural ideals transplanted from the Old World, such social distinctions were soon modified to fit the New World. By the middle of the eighteenth century, a uniquely American social structure had evolved. Class lines were not as sharply drawn as in England, and a person's place in society was determined by a different standard.

In the colonies, wealth came to be the measure of status—not inherited wealth, as was usually the case in England—but acquired wealth. The amount of wealth one needed to be considered "of the better sort" was relative. For example, a man whose estate was worth a hundred pounds would have high status in a community where the average estate was worth only ten pounds. In another community where the average estate was worth a thousand pounds, the same owner's status would be much lower. Opportunities to get rich were much greater in the colonies, however, making movement from class to class swifter and more commonplace.

Because most of the English settlers were middle class, there was no aristocracy, or ruling class, in the colonies as there was in England. In time, however, the colonials developed an aristocracy composed of the elite of colonial society. It differed from the English aristocracy in that its members worked rather than living from the profits of their land (agricultural produce, rents, and so on). This homegrown aristocracy included large landowners like George Washington, wealthy merchants like John Hancock, lawyers like John Adams, and clergymen and government officials.

Some of these prominent colonials were appointed to serve on the royal governors' councils. But there were not enough of these positions to accommodate all who were qualified for leadership roles. As a result, many turned to politics and sought election to the colonial assemblies. These elites were responsible for the power and influence that the assemblies eventually attained.

## "Middling Sort"

Below the colonial elites was a large middle class—the "middling sort," which included farmers, lesser merchants and lawyers, shopkeepers, plantation overseers, and skilled artisans. They did not have education or great wealth, but they had status because they owned property and could vote. When they voted, they usually chose a member of one of the elites to represent them. (Patriot Paul Revere, a silversmith, was one of this middle class.)

The colonial middle class was three times the size of the middle class in England, and the opportunities to move up were more plentiful. The career of Benjamin Franklin—whose father was a candle maker—offers a detailed study in

American upward mobility. Although he ended his days as one of the new country's most distinguished citizens, because his first work was that of a printer, he was originally looked down upon as a social climber, a person "in trade."

## Below the Middle Class

Below the prosperous middle class was a labor force of skilled and unskilled workers and poor frontiersmen. This class also included indentured servants, who in return for paid passage, had agreed to serve a master in one of the colonies for a period of four to five years. Indentured servants came from all levels of English society: Some were farmers and skilled

*The career of Benjamin Franklin remains a good example of the type of upward mobility possible in the New World. Although Franklin's father was a lowly candle maker, Franklin advanced from printer to become one of this nation's most revered citizens.*

workers who had fallen on hard times and hoped to start a new life in the colonies; some were petty criminals. (George Washington's first schoolmaster came to America as an indentured servant.)

An indentured servant's quality of life depended greatly on the master he or she had contracted to serve. Many were accepted as part of the family and served out their terms with dignity. Others were not so fortunate, as is shown in this advertisement in the *Pennsylvania Gazette*, dated January 31, 1760:

> To Be Sold
> A likely *Irish Servant Girl*, who has above five Years and an Half to serve; is fit for Town or Country Business and has had the Small-Pox. Enquire at the New-Printing Office.[18]

But in spite of hardships, the greatest movement upward in status came from immigrants who did not own property but saw the opportunity to do so through hard work and shrewdness.

## Reluctant Immigrants

On the bottom rung were the slaves. The first Africans arrived in the colonies in 1619. But it was not until the end of the seventeenth century, when there was a need for cheap labor, that they were imported in large numbers. At that time the economy in England had improved, and fewer indentured servants were coming to America. Also, some Dutch and American entrepreneurs were finding the slave trade to be highly profitable. Thus slavery came about through greed and what was considered economic necessity.

*Once Americans discovered the profitability of the slave trade, they brought Africans over in great numbers. (Below) The deck of a slave ship reveals the horribly overcrowded conditions Africans endured. (Left) Slaves perform the tedious and backbreaking work of picking cotton.*

The Africans were at a disadvantage from the beginning, having been brought against their will to a new land, and forced to work in a harsh climate. They were strangers to the culture of the New World; and they were physically different, which set them apart. They were also non-Christian, which caused some people to believe that slaves could be treated differently from other people.

## The First Americans

The early colonists saw the Native American (whom they called Indians because of their dark skin) as the "noble savage," pure and unspoiled by civilization. This idealized view soon gave way to an image of the Indians as "barbarians" or "heathens." This image replaced the other when the Native Americans refused to adopt the settlers' customs and religious beliefs. "Savages we call them," wrote Ben-

jamin Franklin, "because their manners differ from ours."[19]

The British and the Native Americans had very different value systems, and their religious beliefs were dissimilar, as well.

*American colonists spent little time trying to understand Native American ways. When colonists found that Indians could not be easily converted to Christianity, they labeled them as inferior and sought to destroy their cultures.*

The Indians believed in a spirit power that was present in nature, but the British, who saw this faith as pagan, considered it their sacred duty to either convert the "heathens" to Christianity or destroy them. Despite efforts by the more enlightened leaders on both sides, the settlers and the Indians were often involved in bitter warfare. Ultimately, Indian tribal life was destroyed.

## Colonial Ideology

Besides the changes in population and the establishment of a social hierarchy, the colonists developed their own political ideas. They still shared many basic political beliefs with the mother country, but by 1763 important exceptions had evolved: exceptions like the representative government that prevailed in all thirteen colonies, and the large number of white adult males who could vote. But there was still agreement on both sides of the Atlantic that too much power in the hands of any person or group would lead to corruption and tyranny. That conviction had, after all, led the English people to revolt against the excessive power of James II in the Glorious Revolution of 1688.

However, it had been a long time since England had felt its liberties threatened by a tyrannical ruler. Once the Glorious Revolution was accomplished, England's democratic fervor over the rights of a free people had faded quickly. But in the colonies, where the people were intensely aware of their rights, the spirit of the Glorious Revolution remained very much alive.

In colonial America, political thinking and writing reflected the ideology of the Whig political party in England. The Whigs advocated limiting the power of the king and increasing the power of Parliament. Much of Whig thought was grounded in the liberal ideals of the English philosopher John Locke. Locke was

## Freedom of the Press

*In 1735, John Peter Zenger, publisher of* the New York Weekly Journal, *printed a criticism of the royal governor of New York and was accused of seditious libel. Zenger was defended at his trial by Andrew Hamilton, an experienced Philadelphia trial lawyer. When the judge denied Hamilton's request to present witnesses to prove the truth of the articles, he appealed directly to the jury. This excerpt is from* A More Perfect Union *edited by Paul F. Boller Jr. and Ronald Story.*

"Gentlemen of the jury, it is to you we must now appeal, for [our] witnesses to the truth . . . we have offered and are denied.

Were you to find a verdict against my client, you must take upon you to say the papers . . . which we acknowledge we printed and published, are false, scandalous and seditious. But of this I have no [fear]. . . . The facts which we offer to prove were not committed in a corner; they are notoriously known to be true; and therefore in your justice lies our safety. And as we are denied the liberty of giving evidence to prove the truth of what we have published, I will beg leave to [say] . . . that the suppressing of evidence ought always to be taken for the strongest evidence; and I hope it will have weight with you. . . .

I hope to be pardoned, sir, for my zeal upon this occasion. It is an old and wise caution that when our neighbor's house is on fire, we ought to take care of our own. For though . . . I live in a government [Pennsylvania] where liberty is well understood, and freely enjoyed, yet experience has shown us all . . . that a bad precedent in one government is soon set up for an authority in another. And therefore I cannot but think . . . we ought . . . to guard against power, wherever we [feel] that it may affect ourselves or our fellow subjects.

I should think it my duty . . . to go to the utmost part of the land . . . to quench the flame of prosecutions . . . set on foot by the governments to deprive a people of the right of [opposing] . . . the [tyrannical] attempts of men in power. Men, who injure and oppress the people under their [government] provoke them to cry out and complain; and then make that very complaint the foundation for new oppressions and prosecutions. I wish I could say there were no instances of this kind."

*Colonists adopted the ideas of English philosopher John Locke to justify their desire for England to play a limited role in American life.*

presses. Although complete freedom of the press did not exist in the prerevolutionary period, there appear to have been few restraints on the open expression of discontent. The first successful colonial newspaper, the *Boston-Newsletter*, was founded in 1704. And the first battle over freedom of the press was fought in the courts in 1735. In that year, John Peter Zenger, publisher of the *New York Weekly Journal*, had printed a criticism of the royal governor of New York. For this he was accused of seditious, or treasonable, libel and imprisoned. Zenger's lawyer argued that no one should be punished for telling the truth, and the jury voted "not guilty."

By 1763, twenty-three newspapers circulated in the colonies. Consisting of only a few pages, these journals and gazettes were published once or twice a week. Many of them reprinted articles written by a group of English Whig writers called the "coffeehouse radicals." In Britain, only a small dissenting fringe accepted the Whig ideology, but they were vocal. These "radicals," as early as 1730, criticized corruption in the English government and warned that English liberties were in jeopardy. Bernard Bailyn describes these writers:

> They insisted, at a time when government was felt to be less oppressive than it had been for two hundred years, that [government] was necessarily—by its very nature—hostile to human liberty and happiness; that . . . it existed only on the tolerance of the people whose needs it served; and that it could be, and reasonably should be, dismissed—overthrown—if it attempted to exceed its proper jurisdiction [bounds].[20]

concerned with maintaining a proper balance between liberty and authority. He believed that a government's only purpose should be to protect the individual's rights to life, liberty, and property. In his *Second Treatise of Government*, written in the early 1680s, he said, in effect, that it was all right to overthrow a corrupt government.

The writings of James Otis and Samuel Adams, and especially Thomas Jefferson's Declaration of Independence, all reflect Lockean philosophy. The colonists often quoted Locke to support their arguments that the colonial policies imposed by Britain in 1763 were unjust and tyrannical.

## Colonial Press

The colonists were well acquainted with the Whig ideology thanks to their printing

American writers learned from the English Whig writers. And in 1763, when Parliament began passing laws that the colonists felt threatened their liberty, American journalists were intellectually prepared to protest and to influence opinion in the colonies.

## Broadsides and Pamphlets

Surpassing newspapers in importance were the broadsides and pamphlets, which appeared everywhere. Broadsides were single sheets of paper that could either be posted or passed from hand to hand. Pamphlets were booklets consisting of printer's sheets folded and loosely stitched together. Much of the most important colonial writing of the American Revolution appeared in pamphlets. It was in this form that "the basic elements of American political thought of the Revolutionary period appeared first."[21]

Newspapers, broadsides, and pamphlets were a powerful force in building up colonial opposition to the British imperialism that followed the French and Indian War. Passed from person to person, these materials were often read aloud in taverns and coffeehouses.

## Collision Course

The colonists, then, were well aware of the importance of protecting their rights against corrupt and power-hungry parties. They resisted, for example, the new policies instituted by Parliament and the king, which they saw as a systematic attack on their fundamental liberties. Nevertheless, they had, as yet, no thought of separating from England.

But England was struggling under a huge national debt, and its overseas possessions cost five times more to govern than had been the case before the French and Indian War. Not surprisingly, the colonies took on new importance as a source of revenue. At the same time, some in England feared that the Americans, who no longer needed protection against the French, might begin thinking of independence. But Benjamin Franklin, who had tried, and failed, to unite the colonies against the French and Indians, expressed the view of most colonials in 1763:

> If [the colonies] could not agree to unite for their defence against the *French* and *Indians*, who were harassing their settlements, burning their villages, and murdering their people, can it reasonably be supposed there is any danger of their uniting against [England], which protects and encourages them . . . and which [it] is well known they all love much more than they love one another? . . . I will venture to say, an union amongst them for such a purpose is not merely improbable, it is impossible.[22]

But Franklin added this warning: "When I say such an union is impossible, I mean without the most grievous tyranny and oppression."[23]

George Grenville, who became England's prime minister in 1763, did not heed the warning. Having inherited an immense national debt, he was determined to make the colonists pay their share.

# 3 England Steps Up Its Control

When the French and Indian War ended, British officials retained a standing army of ten thousand royal troops in North America. The army's purpose, supposedly, was to protect the colonists from Indian raids and from the defeated French—who still kept twenty thousand troops in their Caribbean colonies. The colonists suspected that the army's purpose was to prevent them from expanding to the west, and perhaps to restrain them in other ways. Sharing the traditional Whig fear of peacetime standing armies, the colonists did not want the soldiers in their towns. But they had no say in the matter. They were expected to abide by the decisions of the British administrators in London.

George Grenville, the new prime minister, believed the colonies should always be subordinate to the mother country, obeying without question. Not only was he set on keeping troops in the colonies, he was determined to see that the colonists helped pay for their upkeep.

## The Sugar Act

To achieve his goal, Grenville asked Parliament to approve a bill that would raise money "for defraying the expenses of defending, protecting, and securing the [colonies]."[24] Parliament responded by passing the Sugar Act in 1764. Colonial agents—men we today might call lobbyists, representing the colonies in England—objected to the act, but America's views were never mentioned in parliamentary debate.

The Sugar Act, which replaced the Molasses Act of 1733, was England's first attempt to tax the colonists. The Molasses Act had been designed to regulate trade only. But the Sugar Act's stated purpose was to raise money. It expanded the list of colonial products that could be exported only to England, and it made smuggling more difficult.

Knowing that the colonists had dodged the old Molasses Act through smuggling and by bribing customs officials, Grenville was grimly determined to enforce the Sugar Act. Colonists who violated the law were to be tried in court by a Crown-appointed judge, rather than by a jury of fellow colonists. And violators would be presumed guilty until proven innocent, which was not in accordance with English law.

Some of the colonists saw the Sugar Act as an opening wedge that would lead to more and more taxation. This recorded statement made to the Massachusetts assembly reflects that attitude:

If our trade may be taxed, why not our lands? Why not the produce of our lands and everything we possess or make use of? This we apprehend [understand] annihilates [destroys] our charter right to govern and tax ourselves. It strikes at our British privileges, which, as we have never forfeited them, we hold in common with our fellow subjects who are natives of Britain. If taxes are laid upon us in any shape without ever having a legal representation where they are laid, are we not reduced from the character of free subjects to the miserable state of tributary slaves?[25]

But the majority of the colonists—struggling in a postwar depression—were more upset by the Sugar Act's economic impact than by awareness that it was an indirect tax. The Stamp Act, however, would be a different story.

## Stamps and Rebellion

The hated Stamp Act was a direct tax that required the colonists to pay a surcharge on legal documents such as wills, deeds, and insurance policies. Newspapers, almanacs, broadsides, and pamphlets had to be printed on stamped paper that was taxed. School and college diplomas were taxed. Not even dice and decks of playing cards escaped the tax.

With the passage of the Stamp Act, the colonists felt deprived of their rights as well as their money. They were also bewildered that these new controls came from Parliament, which had always allowed the king and the Board of Trade to direct colonial affairs. Since the Glorious Revolu-

tion, the colonists had regarded Parliament as the protector of their liberties. Suddenly, Parliament seemed more like an oppressor.

No one expressed how the colonists viewed the Stamp Act better than Stephen Johnson. Johnson, who was in his twentieth year as pastor of the First Congregational Church of Lyme, Connecticut, wrote

*Two examples of British stamps made mandatory by the British Stamp Act. Because it was imposed without input from the colonists, the Stamp Act was seen as a blatant violation of their rights.*

six articles that were published in the *New London (Connecticut) Gazette.* If Parliament could impose a stamp tax on America, he said, then it could also impose

> a poll tax, a land tax, a malt tax, a cyder tax, a window tax, a smoke tax, and why not tax us for the light of the sun, the air we breathe, and the ground we are buried in? If they have right to deny us the privilege of tryals by juries, they have as good a right to deny us any tryals at all, and to vote away our estates and lives at pleasure.[26]

Prime Minister Grenville ignored protests the colonies made through their colonial agents (one of whom was Benjamin Franklin) and placed the Stamp Act resolution before Parliament's House of Commons. Charles Townshend, a British statesman, spoke in support of the Stamp Act, commenting sarcastically:

> And now will these Americans, Children planted by our Care, nourished up by our Indulgence until they are grown to a Degree of Strength and Opulence, and protected by our Arms, will they grudge to contribute their mite to relieve us from the heavy weight of that burden which we lie under?[27]

Townshend's statement brought Colonel Isaac Barré, a member of Parliament, to his feet in an impassioned defense of the Americans. Barré had served in the French and Indian War and was a staunch supporter of the colonies. In his emotional reply he coined a phrase that would return to haunt the British, when he referred to the colonists as those "Sons of Liberty."

However, members of Parliament remained unmoved. They refused even to hear the petitions from the colonial assemblies. The Stamp Act passed in March 1765. It would become law in November.

## Sons of Liberty

The news that the Stamp Act had passed reached the colonies in May. The reaction was immediate and violent. In New York, Boston, and other cities, groups calling themselves the Sons of Liberty engaged in open protest. Composed largely of small businessmen, artisans, and laborers—Paul Revere was active in the Boston group—they also included radical intellectuals like Sam Adams, a member of the Massachusetts assembly. Adams played an active role (often behind the scenes) in organizing popular resistance in Boston.

Grenville had hoped to lessen opposition in the colonies by appointing local residents to distribute and collect fees for the stamps. The Sons of Liberty soon "persuaded" these appointees to resign. Their houses were stoned and ransacked. Figures representing stamp distributors were hung in effigy from "liberty trees" throughout the colonies. In Boston, Lieutenant Governor Thomas Hutchinson's mansion was burned and his valuable library destroyed. By November, no one in the colonies was willing to distribute the stamps.

Meanwhile, a less violent group made up of lawyers, printers, and merchants protested through speeches and pamphlets. And at the end of May 1765 an official body, the House of Burgesses in Virginia, took action. Prodded by the young Patrick Henry—who had been a member of the House for only nine

The TIMES are
Dreadful
Doleful
Dismal
Dolorous, and
DOLLAR-LESS.

Thursday, October 31. 1765.

THE

# PENNSYLVANIA JOURNAL;
AND
## WEEKLY ADVERTISER.

NUMB 1195

EXPIRING: In Hopes of a Resurrection to LIFE again.

I am forry to be obliged to acquaint my readers that as the Stamp Act is feared to be obligatory upon us after the *first of November* ensuing (The Fatal To-morrow), The publifher of this paper, unable to bear the Burthen, has thought it expedient to ftop awhile, in order to deliberate, whether any methods can be found to elude the chains forged for us, and efcape the infupportable flavery, which it is hoped, from the laft reprefentation now made againft that act, may be effected. Mean while I muft earneftly Requeft every individual of my Subfcribers, many of whom have been long behind Hand, that they would immediately difcharge their refpective Arrears, that I may be able, not only to fupport myfelf during the Interval, but be better prepared to proceed again with this Paper whenever an opening for that purpofe appears, which I hope will be foon.

WILLIAM BRADFORD.

*The Stamp Act united the colonists in a common desire to force its repeal. At left, a reply to the Stamp Act appears in William Bradford's* Pennsylvania Journal. *Note the caricature of the stamp in the upper right-hand corner. Below, an effigy of a tax collector hangs in a Liberty Tree.*

days—they adopted a set of resolutions known as the Virginia Resolves, denouncing parliamentary taxation. Other colonial assemblies followed Virginia's lead with a speed that demonstrated how united the colonies were in their resistance to the Stamp Act.

## Stamp Act Congress

Massachusetts, recognizing this unity, went a step further. In June, the assembly sent to all the colonies a letter that called for a meeting of colonial representatives to consider what steps should be taken to halt the Stamp Act. As a result, the Stamp Act Congress—the first intercolonial assembly ever summoned by the colonists—met in New York in October 1765. Nine of the

thirteen colonies were represented. The colonies that did not send representatives (New Hampshire, Virginia, North Carolina, and Georgia) sent word through their assemblies that they would agree to whatever was decided by the congress.

This meeting brought together for the first time colonial leaders like James Otis of Massachusetts, Philip Livingston of New York, John Dickinson of Pennsylvania, and Christopher Gadsden of South Carolina. The group drafted a Declaration of Rights and Grievances, to be submitted as a petition to the king and Parliament, asking for a repeal of the Sugar and Stamp Acts. The petition stated in part that "the only representatives of the people of these colonies, are people chosen therein, by themselves; and that no taxes ever have been, or can be constitutionally imposed on them, but by their respective legislatures."[28]

The colonists were determined to get the Stamp Act repealed, or if that failed, to prevent its enforcement. A boycott of English goods had been undertaken half-heartedly in the preceding year when the Sugar Act was passed. Now it would be fully carried out. Merchants agreed to stop importing English goods until the Stamp Act was repealed. This was the beginning of the nonimportation movement: the Patriots themselves did not use the term "boycott" because it was not yet part of the English language.

## Colonies Defy Law

In November when the Stamp Act became official, the colonists united in defiance. The Sons of Liberty, often led by new faces in local politics, forced customs offi-

*James Otis was Massachusetts's delegate to the Stamp Act Congress, which met in New York in 1765 to decide upon a concerted response to the hated act.*

cers to open the ports, and court officials to open the courts, without using the hated stamps. Many merchants closed their shops temporarily, but by late December business proceeded as usual. Newspapers, unstamped, continued to appear weekly urging the people through propaganda and reports of resistance to stand firm. The colonials knew they risked having England descend on them with full military might, but they were willing to take the risk rather than submit to taxation by Parliament, a legislative body in which they were not represented. A shake-up in the British government worked in the colonists' favor.

# Stamp Act Repealed

Before the Stamp Act even became law, Lord Rockingham replaced Grenville as prime minister. Rockingham took office in the summer of 1765, just as news of the unrest in the colonies reached England. And English merchants, feeling the economic pinch of the colonial boycott, immediately besieged the new government to repeal the Stamp Act.

In March 1766, just three months after its passage, Parliament repealed the

---

### "The Cause of *One* is the Cause of *All*"

*John Dickinson, the "penman of the Revolution," who was later a delegate to the Constitutional Convention, was an early defender of colonial rights. His* Letters from a Farmer in Pennsylvania *had great influence in the colonies. This excerpt from his first* Letter *(1767) is taken from* The World of the Founding Fathers, *edited by Saul K. Padover.*

"With a good deal of surprize I have observed that little notice has been taken of an act of parliament, as injurious . . . to the liberties of these colonies, as the Stamp-Act was: I mean the act for suspending the legislation [assembly] of *New-York*.

If the *British* parliament has a legal authority to order, that we shall furnish a single article for the troops here, and to compel obedience to that order; they have the same right to . . . lay *any burdens* they please upon us. If [New York] may be legally deprived . . . of the privilege of making laws, why may they not, with equal reason, be deprived of every other privilege? Or why may not every colony be treated in the same manner?

This . . . suspension . . . is a parliamentary assertion of . . . *supreme authority* . . . over these colonies in *the point of taxation*; and it is intended to COMPEL *New-York* into a submission to that authority. Whoever seriously considers the matter, must perceive, that a dreadful stroke is aimed at the liberty of these colonies. I say of these colonies: For the cause of *one* is the cause of *all*. If the parliament may lawfully deprive *New-York* of any of its rights, it may deprive any, or all the other colonies of their rights; and nothing can possibly so much encourage such attempts, as a mutual inattention to the interest of each other. When the slightest point touching the freedom of a single colony is agitated, I earnestly wish, that all the rest may . . . support their sister."

Stamp Act without having collected any money from its provisions. But even while the colonists celebrated—ringing church bells, firing cannon salutes, and setting off fireworks—the more thoughtful ones were experiencing gnawing doubts about another bill that Parliament had passed in conjunction with the repeal. That bill, the Declaratory Act, stated in very vague terms Parliament's right "to make laws and statutes . . . to bind the colonies . . . in all cases whatsoever."[29] Did "in all cases whatsoever" include taxation? In Boston John Adams questioned "whether [England] will lay a tax in consequence of that resolution."[30] Another change in the British government would soon provide the answer.

## Noble Sons of Liberty

*In* The Glorious Cause, *Robert Middlekauff quotes Isaac Barré's defense of the colonies made in response to Charles Townshend's belittling remarks. The speech, given during the Stamp Act debate in Parliament, made Barré a popular figure in America.*

"They [the colonies] planted by your Care? No! your Oppressions planted [them] in America. They fled from your Tyranny to a then uncultivated and unhospitable Country—where they exposed themselves to almost all the Cruelties of a Savage foe. And yet, actuated by Principles of true english Lyberty, they met all these hardships with pleasure, compared with those they suffered in their own Country, from the hands of those who should have been their Friends.

They nourished up by your indulgence? they grew by your neglect of [them]: as soon as you began to care about [them], that Care was Exercised in sending persons to rule over [them], . . . who were perhaps the Deputies of Deputies to some Member of this house—sent to Spy out their Lyberty, to misrepresent their Actions and to prey upon [them]; men whose behaviour on many Occasions has caused the Blood of those Sons of Liberty to recoil within them.

They protected by *your* Arms? they have nobly taken up Arms in your Defence, . . . for the defence of a Country, whose frontier, while drench'd in blood, . . . yielded all its little Savings to your Emolument [advantage]. And believe me, remember I this Day told you so, that same Spirit of freedom which actuated that people at first will accompany them still."

# The Townshend Acts

In what looked like another break for the colonies, Prime Minister Rockingham was replaced by William Pitt. Pitt, who was secretary of state during the French and Indian War, was well liked in the colonies because of his handling of that war, and because he had strongly opposed the Stamp Act. But by the time of his appointment in 1766, Pitt was seriously ill, and Charles Townshend, the chancellor of the exchequer, or royal treasurer, became the acting prime minister.

Charles Townshend was no friend of the Americans. He believed in full parliamentary authority over the colonies. And he had been a force behind the Declaratory Act. In June 1767 he introduced a bill calling for new customs duties on colonial products that, according to the longstanding Navigation Acts, could not be obtained unless they were imported from England. The products included glass, lead, paints, paper, and tea.

Townshend hoped to collect enough money not only to pay for defense, but also to pay the salaries of royal governors and judges in the colonies. In that way the royal officials would be independent of the colonial assemblies, who currently controlled and paid their salaries. This would take power away from the assemblies. Without control of the purse strings, the assemblies would have no leverage for bargaining with the royal governors. The first of the Townshend Acts became effective November 20, 1767. Other laws in the series followed.

The colonists were slow to react to the Townshend Acts because there was no visible symbol, like the stamps, to serve as a focus of agitation. But the customs officers who arrived from England on November 5, 1767, were highly visible. They had come armed with the authority to issue search warrants to look for smuggled goods, "to enter and go into any house, warehouse, shop, cellar, or other place in the British colonies . . . in America to search for and seize prohibited . . . goods."[31] In a policy sure to lead to corruption, the customs commissioners were to be paid out of the fines they collected from smugglers. The commissioners would also receive one-third of the total value of every ship and cargo caught violating British law.

To make matters worse, the British army had been called back from western outposts to ensure order in the ports. The colonists were required by the Quartering Act, passed in 1765, to provide living quarters for these soldiers in unoccupied buildings if no barracks or inns were available. In 1768, when the New York assembly refused to vote the necessary funds to feed and house the British troops, the royal governor ordered the colonial legislature to pass the bill. But New York stood firm, and Parliament then ordered the assembly dissolved.

# "Patriotic 92"

Meanwhile in Massachusetts, the colonists were beginning to understand the full meaning of the Townshend Acts. On February 11, 1768, the Massachusetts assembly sent a letter to all the colonial assemblies protesting the Townshend Acts. The letter, written by Sam Adams and James Otis, attacked the plan to use customs duties to

# Resolves of the Virginia House of Burgesses

*In June 1765, the House of Burgesses accepted four of Patrick Henry's seven proposed resolutions against the Stamp Act. These statements, the Virginia Resolves, expressing the principles that would lead to the American Revolution, are taken from* U.S. Colonial History, Readings and Documents, *edited by David Hawke.*

"That the first adventurers and settlers of this his Majesty's colony . . . brought with them, and transmitted to their posterity [descendants] . . . all the liberties, privileges, franchises, and immunities that at any time have been held, enjoyed, and possessed by the people of Great Britain.

That by two royal charters, granted by King James the First, the colonies . . . are declared entitled to all liberties, privileges and immunities . . . as if they had been abiding and born within the realm of England.

*Resolved, therefore*, that the General Assembly of this colony . . . have the sole right . . . to lay taxes and impositions upon its inhabitants. And that every attempt to [place] such authority in any other person or persons whatsoever has a manifest tendency to destroy American freedom.

That his Majesty's [loyal subjects] . . . of this colony, are not bound to yield obedience to any law . . . whatsoever designed to impose any taxation upon them, other than the laws or ordinances of the General Assembly. . . .

That any person who shall, by speaking or writing, assert . . . that any person or persons other than the General Assembly of this colony . . . have any right or authority to . . . impose any tax whatever on the inhabitants thereof, shall be [considered] an enemy to this his Majesty's colony."

*Patrick Henry had been a member of the House of Burgesses for only nine days when four of his seven proposed resolutions were adopted to protest the Stamp Act.*

pay royal officials as being unconstitutional. It also called for a boycott of British imports. Largely in response to the Massachusetts circular letter, one after another of the colonial assemblies voted to stop importing English goods until the Townshend Acts were repealed.

Under instructions from Parliament, Massachusetts governor Francis Bernard ordered the Massachusetts assembly to rescind the letter, saying that failure to do so would result in the assembly's being dismissed. By a vote of 92 to 17, the assembly refused to withdraw the letter, and as promised, the legislature was dissolved.

Still the colony continued to be defiant. Sam Adams and Sons of Liberty everywhere adopted the slogan "Patriotic 92," honoring the majority voters who had refused to recall the letter. Paul Revere, silversmith, designed and made a silver punch bowl dedicated to the "Immortal 92." The Sons of Liberty also began a drive to remove from office the seventeen who had voted to rescind the letter. Seven of the seventeen lost their assembly seats in the next election. As the Sons of Liberty continued to flex their muscles, they received support from unlikely sources.

## Redcoats in Boston

Thirty-one-year-old John Hancock, soon to be elected to the Massachusetts assembly, was a generous supporter of the Sons of Liberty in Boston. He contributed money for printing handbills, for banners, and

*Leading member of the Sons of Liberty, Sam Adams cowrote a letter with James Otis that demanded the repeal of the Townshend Acts.*

for free rum at rallies. So in the summer of 1768 when the despised customs officials seized Hancock's sloop *Liberty*, on a false charge of having smuggled goods aboard, they were mobbed by an angry Boston crowd.

This action brought an unwanted response. Two regiments of royal troops were dispatched from Nova Scotia and two more from England. Their purpose was to bring Boston into submission as an example to the rest of the colonies. On October 1, 1768, the red-coated troops marched into Boston without meeting resistance.

# 4 Propelled Toward Revolution

Many Bostonians, including Sam Adams and James Otis, advocated using force to keep British troops out of Boston. Hoping to unite Massachusetts in this effort, Boston had called on the other towns to send delegates to an unofficial convention. The convention met, but the majority of its delegates were unwilling to resort to force.

However, it was significant that towns much more conservative than Boston sent representatives to a convention that England considered to be unlawful. Moreover, the convention demonstrated that the people would not be prevented from speaking through their representatives, even though the royal governor had dissolved the regular assembly. The convention adjourned on October 1, the same day British warships anchored in Boston Harbor with guns aimed at the town.

## Lobsterbacks

Although Boston offered no resistance, relations between soldiers and civilians were tense from the outset. Street fights and brawls in taverns were common. The soldiers took over a number of public buildings for barracks. They used the Boston Common, land that had been set aside for use by all Bostonians, as a campground. They paraded on Sunday morning, disrupting church services with their drills and drums. The citizens of Boston maintained a rigid restraint to keep violence in check, but they set out to make the soldiers as uncomfortable as possible.

Townspeople meeting soldiers on the streets treated them with contempt. Children followed them, ridiculing their red uniforms with taunts of "lobsterbacks" and "bloody-backs." To earn extra money, the underpaid soldiers often took second jobs during their off-duty hours. Boston's working class resented this additional competition for jobs. They harassed the soldiers verbally and sometimes physically, but the harassment always stopped just short of endangering life.

The soldiers were handicapped by strict orders that they were never to fire upon citizens of the city or to attack them in any other way, except on the order of an officer. And officers could not call out troops against civilians without a written order from a civil authority, which would be difficult to obtain.

By the summer of 1769, the British government realized that the troops were serving no useful purpose in Boston. The British commander, General Thomas Gage, agreed in the following words:

The people were as Lawless and Licentious [unruly] after the Troops arrived, as they were before. The Troops could not act by Military Authority, and no Persons in Civil Authority would ask their aid. They were there contrary to the wishes of the Council, Assembly, Magistrates and People, and seemed only offered to abuse and Ruin. And the Soldiers were either to suffer ill usage and even assaults upon their Persons till their Lives were in Danger, or by resisting and defending themselves, to run almost a Certainty of suffering by the Law.[32]

Bostonians were overjoyed when two British regiments left Boston for Canada. They assumed the other two regiments would soon follow. When they didn't, tension increased and the citizens grew more and more hostile. Something had to give.

## The Bloody Massacre Perpetrated in King Street

The night of March 5, 1770, was crisp and cold. The crunch of Bostonian boots on the foot of snow covering the ground would have carried a far distance through the clear night air. On King Street, Private Hugh White stood guard before the Customs House.

At 9:00 P.M. a seemingly spontaneous crowd gathered, taunting and threatening the lone sentry. He shouted for help. A squad of nine Redcoats, including Captain Thomas Preston, the officer of the day, joined him. The crowd continued to hurl insults and snowballs at the soldiers. Suddenly someone yelled, "Fire!"

Several witnesses thought they heard Captain Preston give the command. Oth-

*In Paul Revere's sensationalized drawing of the Boston Massacre, grinning redcoats purposely fire on unarmed colonists. The massacre further hardened the hearts of the colonists against compromise with the British.*

ers were certain they saw shots fired from the windows of the Customs House. It was never established who gave the command, but when the smoke cleared, three Bostonians were dead and eight wounded. Two of the wounded died later. No shots had been fired at the soldiers.

At the sound of the shots, the streets filled with alarmed citizens. Riders were sent to neighboring towns asking for help against the army. The people disbursed only when the acting governor, Thomas Hutchinson, ordered Captain Preston and the eight soldiers imprisoned to await trial. He also ordered that all soldiers be removed from the town to Castle William, a fort on an island in Boston Harbor.

## Redcoats on Trial

Infuriated by the killings, the people of Boston wanted the soldiers tried and executed immediately. However, they doubted that there was a lawyer in Boston who would risk defending them. Two were willing: Patriots John Adams and Josiah Quincy. In his closing speech at the trial, Adams appealed to the jury:

We talk much of *Liberty and property*. But if we cut up the law of self-defense, we cut away the foundation of both. Place yourself in the situation of . . . the sentry. . . . The people are crying, Kill them! kill them! knock them down!— heaving snow balls, oyster shells, clubs, white birch sticks three and a half inches in diameter. . . . Consider yourselves in this situation and then judge if a reasonable man would not consider they were gong to kill him.[33]

*A colonial broadside lists the names of Americans who died or were wounded during the Boston Massacre.*

AMERICANS!
BEAR IN REMEMBRANCE
The HORRID MASSACRE!
Perpetrated in King-ftreet, Boston,
New-England,
On the Evening of March the Fifth, 1770.
When FIVE of your fellow countrymen,
GRAY, MAVERICK, CALDWELL, ATTUCKS,
and CARR,
Lay wallowing in their Gore!
Being *bafely*, and moft *inhumanly*
MURDERED!
And SIX others badly WOUNDED!
By a Party of the XXIXth Regiment,
Under the command of Capt. Tho. Preston.
REMEMBER!
That Two of the MURDERERS
Were convicted of MANSLAUGHTER!
By a Jury, of whom I fhall fay
NOTHING,
Branded in the hand!
And *difmiffed*,
The others were ACQUITTED,
And their Captain PENSIONED!
Alfo,
BEAR IN REMEMBRANCE
That on the 22d Day of February, 1770
The infamous
EBENEZER RICHARDSON, Informer,
And tool to Minifterial hirelings,
Moft *barbaroufly*
MURDERED
CHRISTOPHER SEIDER,
An innocent youth!
Of which crime he was found guilty
By his Country
On Friday April 20th, 1770;
But remained *Unfentenced*
On Saturday the 22d Day of February, 1772.
When the GRAND INQUEST
For Suffolk county,
Were informed, at requeft,
By the Judges of the Superior Court,
That EBENEZER RICHARDSON'S *Cafe*
Then *lay before his* MAJESTY.
Therefore faid *Richardfon*
This day, MARCH FIFTH! 1772,
Remains UNHANGED!!!
Let THESE things be told to Pofterity!
And handed down
From Generation to Generation,
'Till Time fhall be no more!
Forever may AMERICA be preferved,
From weak and wicked monarchs,
Tyrannical Minifters,
Abandoned Governors,
Their Underlings and Hirelings!
And may the
Machinations of artful, *defigning* wretches,
Who would ENSLAVE THIS People,
Come to an end,
Let their NAMES and MEMORIES
Be buried in eternal oblivion,
And the PRESS,
For a *SCOURGE* to Tyrannical Rulers,
Remain FREE.

*John Adams defended the soldiers brought to trial after the Boston Massacre. Adams thought it would assure his political demise, yet his actions brought him greater respect.*

Captain Preston and six of the soldiers were acquitted. The other two were convicted of manslaughter. They both pleaded benefit of clergy—a technicality used at the time to avoid the death penalty. The convicted soldiers were branded on the thumbs with a hot iron to mark them as convicts and discharged.

That these British soldiers received a fair trial in a town that was boiling over with anger and resentment ranks as one of the finest accomplishments in American history. Sam Adams lamented that his cousin, John, would be forced to give up his law practice and any chance of a career in politics after defending such an unpopular cause. John Adams agreed. But as the tempers of the townspeople cooled, they began to feel a new respect for John

Adams's courage. He was elected to the Massachusetts assembly by a large majority and would go on to become the second president of the United States.

## Repeal of Townshend Acts

In a strange coincidence, on the same day as the Boston Massacre, Parliament—led by Lord North, the new prime minister— voted to repeal all the Townshend duties except for the tax on tea. King George III, who ascended the throne in 1760 (during the French and Indian War) had a total of six prime ministers in his first decade as king. With each one, the gap between the mother country and her colonies had widened. Lord North, a favorite of the king's, would complete the separation.

*Prime Minister Lord North voted to repeal all the Townshend duties except for the tax on tea.*

# A Colonist's Account of the Boston Massacre

*John Tudor, a justice of the peace in Boston, wrote an entry in his diary about the Boston Massacre as he saw it. David Hawke includes it in* U.S. Colonial History, Readings and Documents.

"On Monday evening, the 5th [of March], a few minutes after nine o'clock, a most horrid murder was committed in King Street before the customs house door by eight or nine soldiers under the command of Captain Thomas Preston. . . .

This unhappy affair began by some boys and young fellows throwing snowballs at the sentry placed at the customs house door. On which eight or nine soldiers came to his assistance. Soon after a number of people collected, when the captain commanded the soldiers to fire, which they did, and three men were killed on the spot and several mortally wounded, one of which died the next morning. [A fifth man died several days later.] The captain soon drew off his soldiers . . . or the consequences might have been terrible, for on the guns firing the people were alarmed and set the bells a-ringing as if for fire, which drew multitudes to the place of action.

*Dramatic depictions of the Boston Massacre such as this one further fueled anti-British sentiment.*

Lieutenant Governor Hutchinson, who was commander-in-chief, was sent for and came to the council chamber. . . . The governor [asked] the multitude about ten o'clock to separate and go home peaceable, and he would do all in his power that justice should be done, etc. . . . But the people insisted that the soldiers should be ordered to their barracks first before they would separate. Which being done, the people separated about one o'clock. Captain Preston was taken up by a warrant . . . and we sent him to jail soon after three, having evidence sufficient to commit him, on his ordering his soldiers to fire. So about four o'clock the town became quiet."

However, the Boston Massacre and the subsequent removal of soldiers from within the city temporarily released some of the tension in Boston. And the repeal of the Townshend Acts, along with reinstatement of the dissolved assemblies, brought a period of relative calm throughout all the colonies in the years 1770–1772.

# Burning of the *Gaspee*

In June 1772, the peaceful interlude (uneasy at best) ceased. The British navy had placed several warships at the disposal of the customs commissioners. Commanding one of these ships, the *Gaspee*, was Lieutenant William Dudingston. While cruising in Narragansett Bay he had been harassing farmers and fishermen, often disregarding the colonists' rights in his zeal to stop the smuggling in Rhode Island. On June 9, 1772, while pursuing a merchant ship suspected of smuggling, the *Gaspee* ran aground near Providence.

The following night eight boatloads of men—led by wealthy Providence merchant John Brown—boarded the *Gaspee*, wounded the lieutenant, and burned the ship. England was furious that her own subjects had attacked a ship of the Royal Navy. A full-scale investigation was ordered, and a reward was offered for identification of the vandals. But even though there had been many eyewitnesses, not a person in Rhode Island came forward. Threatened with loss of charter, Rhode Island apologized for the incident. England decided that the action had been the work of a handful of hooligans and accepted the apology.

Following the *Gaspee* incident, England once again focused on Massachu-setts, considered to be the ringleader of colonial unrest. Trying to gain more control in the colonies and to halt the kind of civil disobedience that had occurred in Rhode Island, the Crown announced that customs revenues would be used to pay the salaries of the royal governor of Massachusetts and of the colony's superior court judges. These salaries formerly had been paid by the Massachusetts assembly, which had used the threat of withholding salaries as a bargaining tool when dealing with the Crown-appointed officials. Now the colonial legislators lost that power. And as the British government extended the new practice to other colonies—putting one governor and judge after another on the royal payroll—radical political leaders like Sam Adams grew increasingly uneasy. Adams felt that unless something was done, colonial liberties would be completely destroyed, and one day the colonists would find themselves helplessly under the control of royal officials. In desperation, Massachusetts Patriots sought an effective way to protest this erosion of colonial rights.

# Committees of Correspondence

In October, Sam Adams came up with a brilliant idea. One that would unite the colonies. He organized some fellow Patriots into a group called the Committee of Correspondence, to prepare a list of violations of colonial rights. The list was to be circulated among the other Massachusetts towns. Those towns, in turn, were encouraged to prepare and circulate their own lists of abuses. "It is natural to suppose,"

Benjamin Franklin wrote to Thomas Cushing, the speaker of the Massachusetts assembly, "that if the oppressions continue, a congress may grow out of that correspondence."[34]

The Boston committee produced its first report (written by Sam Adams) on November 20. Response was instantaneous. By the end of 1772, eighty Massachusetts towns had created Committees of Correspondence. The idea soon spread from Massachusetts to other colonies. And in March 1773, the Virginia House of Burgesses proposed an intercolonial committee. By summertime all but three colonies had correspondence committees. They waited for Parliament's next move, ready to work together if there were any further violations of colonial rights. They didn't have long to wait.

## Tempest in a Teacup

The colonies' next grievance would center around a favorite colonial beverage, tea. The British East India Company had held a monopoly over all trade between India and the British Empire for almost 175 years. But the colonial boycott had taken its toll. By the 1770s the company had a huge backlog of tea stored in its warehouses and faced bankruptcy.

The colonists still imported some East India tea, but because of the remaining Townshend tax on tea, they smuggled in large amounts from Holland. Prime Minister North devised a plan to save the East India Company from bankruptcy.

The East India Company had been required by English law to auction its tea to English wholesale merchants—who in turn sold it to colonial American wholesale merchants. Under Lord North's Tea Act, which Parliament passed in May 1773, the company could bypass American wholesale merchants and appoint its own agents to distribute tea directly to colonial retailers. In this way the East India Company could undersell the smuggled tea. Parliament could just as easily have lowered the price by removing the Townshend duty on tea. But Lord North refused to remove the tax even though several members of Parliament warned that the colonists wouldn't buy the tea—no matter how cheap it was—as long as it carried the tax.

The Tea Act stirred up the old issue of taxation without representation. The Boston Committee of Correspondence immediately sent letters to the other colonies. The letters warned that by lowering the price of tea without removing the duty, Parliament was trying to trick them into accepting the unconstitutional Townshend tax.

## Tea Party in Boston

The tea began arriving in American ports in November 1773. Reminiscent of colonial reaction to the Stamp Act, resistance to the Tea Act was almost unanimous. East India agents were harassed in every port. Dockworkers in New York, Philadelphia, and Massachusetts refused to unload the tea. New York and Philadelphia sent the tea ships back to England. However the governor of Massachusetts was determined that the tea would be unloaded and the duty paid. Thomas Hutchinson, who now held that office, refused to grant the tea ships clearance papers for their return to England.

On December 16 broadsides were posted in public places by the Boston Patriots:

Friends! brethren! countrymen!— That worst of plagues, the detested tea, shipped for this port by the East India Company, is now arrived in this harbour—the hour of destruction or manly opposition to the machinations of tyranny stare you in the face. Every friend to his country, to himself, and posterity, is now called upon to meet at Faneuill Hall, at nine o'clock *this day*, at which time the bells will ring, to make an united and successful resistance to this last, worst, and most destructive measure of administration.[35]

Five thousand people responded to the notice. Too large for Faneuill Hall, the crowd moved to the Old South Church. Urgent messages had been sent to Governor Hutchinson, requesting that the tea ships be allowed to return to England. The crowd waited for an answer. Word finally came that the governor had no intention of granting the request. "This

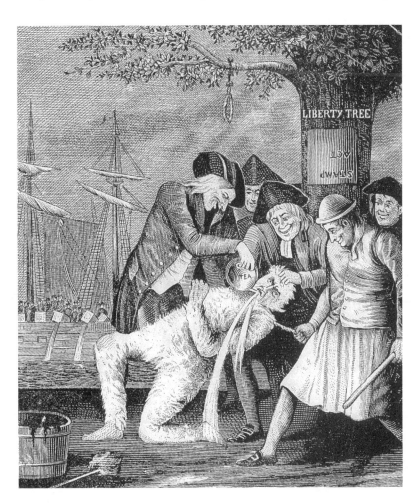

*In this eighteenth-century cartoon, Bostonians force tea down a tarred-and-feathered tax collector's throat to protest the tea tax.*

meeting," Sam Adams told the crowd, "can do no more to save the country."[36]

That evening thirty to sixty Sons of Liberty, lightly disguised as Mohawk Indians, made their way to Griffin's Wharf. Boarding the three British ships—the *Beaver*, the *Eleanor*, and the *Dartmouth*—they dumped forty-five tons of tea into Boston Harbor. No other part of the ship's cargo was touched.

Historian Page Smith remarks on the disciplined behavior demonstrated in the dumping of the tea:

> Measured against the dangerous . . . violence occasioned by the Stamp Act, or against the uncontrolled violence of the rioters on the night of the Boston Massacre, the Tea Party showed . . .

how far the patriot cause had come from its tumultuous beginnings some eight years before. By now the patriot leaders had established firm control. There were no rioters among the carefully drilled Mohawks who dumped the tea in Boston Harbor; they were rather a corps of irregulars who might, on the next occasion carry loaded muskets. But if they did so it would be in response to orders, not to the volatile [explosive] passions of a mob.[37]

## Pride and Consequences

Regarding the Tea Party, a young John Adams wrote in his diary:

*Colonists dressed as Mohawks dump dozens of crates of tea into Boston Harbor to protest the Tea Act.*

## Rallying Song of the Tea Party

*Many prominent Patriots such as Sam Adams and John Hancock took part in the Boston Tea Party. Paul Revere, the midnight rider, is mentioned in this song, as is Dr. Joseph Warren. The song, written by an unknown colonial poet, is quoted in Esther Forbes's classic* Paul Revere and the World He Lived In.

Rally Mohawks! bring out your axes,
And tell King George we'll pay no taxes
  On his foreign tea;
His threats are vain, and vain to think
To force our girls and wives to drink
  His vile Bohea!
Then rally, boys, and hasten on
To meet our chiefs at the Green Dragon.

Our Warren's there and bold Revere,
With hands to do, and words to cheer,
  For liberty and laws;
Our country's "braves" and firm defenders
Shall ne'er be left by true North-Enders
  Fighting Freedom's cause!
Then rally, boys, and hasten on
To meet our chiefs at the Green Dragon.

This is the most significant movement of all. There is a dignity, a majesty . . . in this last effort of the patriots that I greatly admire. This destruction of the tea is so bold, so daring, so firm, . . . and it must have important consequences.[38]

The "consequences" were not long in coming. When news of the destruction of the tea reached England, Parliament and the Crown responded with anger and vengeance. "The dye is now cast," King George wrote to Lord North. "The colonies must either submit or triumph."[39]

Debates regarding the tea incident began in the House of Commons on March 14, 1774. Lord North, calling for swift punishment, told the Commons that "Boston had been the ringleader in all riots, and had at all times shewn a desire of seeing the laws of Great Britain attempted in vain in the colony of Massachusetts Bay.[40]

## Intolerable Acts

Parliament responded to Lord North's call for action by passing four laws that Bostonians promptly labeled the Intolerable Acts. The first, the Boston Port Bill, closed Massachusetts's principal harbor to all shipping until the citizens had both compensated the East India Company for the lost tea and paid the required tax.

A week later Parliament passed the Massachusetts Government Act. Under this act, the royal governor no longer had to work with an elective council whose members were chosen annually by the assembly. The council would now be chosen by the king. And the governor received enormous new powers—he could even ban town meetings. In effect, this act revoked the Massachusetts charter, which the citizens treasured as their guarantee of liberty.

A third bill, the Administration of Justice Act, passed on the same day as the Government Act. Under the Justice Act, any government officials who were charged with committing violence while suppressing a riot or any other disturbance would be tried in England.

The final Intolerable Act expanded on the old Quartering Act. Troops could now be housed in occupied private homes. Unlike the other acts, which applied only to Massachusetts, this one applied to all colonies.

## Colonies Support Boston

The Intolerable Acts were meant to intimidate the other colonies by making an example of Massachusetts, but the plan backfired. Instead, the colonies saw Boston as a mistreated martyr standing bravely in defense of colonial rights. They sent supplies and wrote encouraging letters through their Committees of Correspondence, pledging to stop all trade with England and declaring that "all Americans must resolve to stand by one another even unto the position of death."[41]

By June 1774, Boston was once again occupied by British troops, and Massachusetts had a military governor. King George had appointed General Gage, the commander in chief of British forces in America, to replace Hutchinson. Reeling from England's harsh punishments and fearful of losing all her liberties, Massachusetts called for an intercolonial congress. All colonies immediately began electing delegates to represent them at this gathering.

# 5 Colonies Begin to Unite

British leaders had never doubted their ability to control the thirteen colonies. They were confident that the colonies could not stop quarreling with one another and become united. Consequently, they were alarmed by the possibility of the colonies coming together at a continental congress. Royal governors even tried to prevent the colonists from electing delegates to the forthcoming meeting by declaring their colonial assemblies illegal. But the assembly members continued to meet anyway.

The Virginia House of Burgesses met at the Raleigh Tavern in Williamsburg and conducted business as usual. On May 27, 1774, they announced that "an attack made on one of our sister colonies . . . is an attack made on all British America, and threatens ruin to the rights of all."[42] Other colonies organized unlawful local, or provincial, congresses or county conventions in order to choose their delegates. Colonial leaders, without realizing it, were preparing for a revolution. Only in Georgia did a royal governor succeed in blocking the naming of delegates.

Fifty-five colonial delegates gathered in Philadelphia in September 1774 for the First Continental Congress. They met, not to consider a break with England, but to assert their rights and try to restore a friendly relationship with the mother country. Every colony except Georgia sent at least one delegate.

## Conservatives and Radicals

The First Continental Congress was divided into two groups: conservatives and radicals. Members in both groups ranged from moderate to extreme.

The conservatives urged restraint and wanted compromise and reconciliation with England. They were called Tories. Extreme conservatives would later become active supporters of England during the years of the Revolutionary War and would call themselves Loyalists because they retained their allegiance to England.

The radicals did not want complete separation from England either, but they wanted action. They urged defiance and a united resistance against the unconstitutional acts of Parliament. The radicals were called Whigs or Patriots. John Adams described the makeup of the Congress as "one-third Tories, another [third] Whigs, and the rest Mongrels."[43]

The one thing all the delegates agreed on was the need to support Massachusetts against Britain's harsh treatment. But they differed over what methods to use. And there was still distrust among the different groups of settlers.

Boston had a radical reputation throughout the colonies. That meant that the Massachusetts delegates (John and

---

## Kings Are the Servants of the People

*Thomas Jefferson was serving in the Virginia House of Burgesses when he wrote "A Summary View of the Rights of British America." His first published work, meant only to serve as a guide for Virginia delegates elected to the First Continental Congress, it was reprinted many times in both England and America. This excerpt is from the biography* Jefferson *by Saul K. Padover.*

"Can any one reason be assigned why 160,000 electors in the island of Great Britain should give law to four millions in the States of America, every individual of whom is equal to every individual of them . . . ? Were this to be [allowed], instead of being a free people, as we have hitherto supposed, and mean to continue [to be], we should suddenly be found the slaves not of one but of 160,000 tyrants.

But can his majesty . . . put down all law under his feet? Can he erect a power superior to that which erected himself? He has done it indeed by force, but let him remember that force cannot give right.

. . . These are our grievances which we have thus laid before his majesty, with that freedom of language and sentiment which becomes a free people claiming their rights, as derived from the laws of nature, and not as the gift of their chief magistrate. Let those flatter who fear[;] it [flattery] is not an American art. . . . [We] know . . . that kings are the servants, not the proprietors of the people.

It is neither our wish nor our interest to separate from [Great Britain]. We are willing, on our part, to sacrifice everything which reason can ask to the restoration of . . . tranquility. . . . On their part, let them be ready to establish union on a generous plan. . . . But let them not think to exclude us from . . . other markets. . . . Still less it be proposed that our properties within our own territories shall be taxed or regulated by any power on earth but our own.

The God who gave us life gave us liberty at the same time: the hand of force may destroy, but cannot disjoin them. This, sire, is our last, our determined resolution."

Sam Adams, Thomas Cushing, James Bowdoin, and Robert Treat Paine) had to convince the Congress that New Englanders could be trusted. This was so important that Joseph Hawley, the leading Patriot in western Massachusetts, wrote the delegation before they left for Philadelphia to caution them on their behavior.

## Behind the Scenes

The Massachusetts delegates especially needed to win congressional support against the Government Act that had deprived them of their charter, and they needed help to get British troops out of Boston. They began gathering that support on the way to Philadelphia. They made stops in Connecticut, New York, and New Jersey to meet with both Tory and Patriot leaders.

The Massachusetts group also arrived in Philadelphia a week early to talk with other delegates before the Congress met. This strategy enabled the New Englanders to form tentative alliances and to sound out the feelings of individual delegates. John Adams wrote to William Tudor, his wife's cousin, that he and his colleagues were "obliged to act with great delicacy and caution, to keep ourselves out of sight, and to feel pulses, and to sound the depths; to insinuate [communicate] our sentiments, designs, and desires, by means of other persons, sometimes of one province [colony], and sometimes of another."[44]

The most important of these informal meetings was with the Virginia delegation. Any resistance against Parliament and the king would require a strong alliance between Virginia and Massachusetts, the two colonies that had always been the leaders in opposition. Yet the two were so different in character that such an alliance seemed improbable.

The lighthearted, aristocratic Virginians and the somber, thrifty New Englanders had little in common. Virginia was run by plantation owners—the equivalent of English country gentlemen—and its economy was based on the institution of slavery. Massachusetts, the birthplace of American Puritanism, was a middle-class society run by lawyers and merchants, and the economy was based on small, self-sufficient farms and trade. The only thing the two colonies had in common, other than their English heritage, was a determination to keep their American freedoms intact. In the end, that was enough.

John Adams wrote in his diary: "These gentlemen from Virginia appear to be the most spirited and consistent, of any [of the delegates]."[45]

## Congress Is in Session

The First Continental Congress held its opening session on September 5 in Carpenters' Hall, a private building owned by the Carpenters' Guild [union] of Philadelphia. Peyton Randolph, a political moderate from Virginia, and a member of the House of Burgesses since 1748, was elected president of the Congress. His election was unanimous, probably because of his moderate views. Still, the radicals considered it a victory to have a Virginian chairing the proceedings.

Charles Thomson, who had been active in the nonimportation movement in

*Charles Thomson's call for nonimportation. Thomson's election as secretary for the first Continental Congress was praised by the radicals and criticized by the conservatives.*

1770, was elected secretary. A leader of Philadelphia's Sons of Liberty, he was called "the Sam Adams of Philadelphia." His election was clearly a triumph for the radicals, and the conservatives grumbled that the election had been "privately settled" before Congress convened.

The Congress set itself three objectives: to compose a statement of colonial rights, to list Parliament's violations of those rights, and to provide a plan that would persuade England to restore those rights. But first the question of how to vote had to be decided—whether by one vote to a colony or by head count.

Virginia, being large, wanted to vote by head count. Patrick Henry spoke for the Virginia delegates. "The distinctions between Virginians, Pennsylvanians, New Yorkers, and New Englanders are no more," he said. "I am not a Virginian but an American."[46] However, the smaller colonies with fewer delegates wanted to vote by colony. Finally John Jay, a moder-

ate conservative from New York, moved that the Congress give one vote to each colony—with an official notation that this solution was only a temporary, working arrangement. The motion was accepted. It was another step toward unity. The delegates were putting aside provincial differences to serve the higher cause.

## Rumors and Resolves

On the second day of the Congress, an express rider arrived from Boston with the news that royal troops had raided the weapons storehouses at Charlestown and Cambridge, Massachusetts. In addition, a false rumor that five colonists had been killed and Boston itself bombarded had caused thousands of militiamen to march from outlying rural areas to defend the city. This "Powder Alarm," and the Massachusetts countryside's quick response to it, added another item to the congressional agenda. Delegates would also discuss how far Massachusetts should go in resisting the British troops.

That matter took center stage on September 16 when Paul Revere, having ridden night and day, arrived from Massachusetts with the Suffolk Resolves. The seizure of the gunpowder had resulted in a convention of outraged delegates from Suffolk County, which included Boston. The convention, taking over the role of the suspended Massachusetts assembly, had drawn up the Suffolk Resolves.

Drafted by Dr. Joseph Warren, the document declared the Intolerable Acts to be unconstitutional and stated that "no obedience is due from this province to . . . any part of the acts."[47] Massachusetts was urged to form an independent government until the acts were repealed. The Resolves also advised the people to arm themselves and advocated economic sanctions against Great Britain, Ireland, and the West Indies—no products to be imported or exported.

Although the Suffolk Resolves contained the strongest statements yet made against England, the Continental Congress endorsed them—even breaking into applause after they were read before the Congress. That night, John Adams wrote: "This was one of the happiest Days of my life. . . . This Day convinced me that America will support the Massachusetts [colony] or perish with her."[48]

Joseph Galloway, the conservative delegate from New York—who would later become a Loyalist—called the Suffolk Resolves "a declaration of war against Great Britain."[49] On September 28, Galloway, with the conservative delegates united behind him, introduced his own resolves for a *Political Union Between the Colonies and the Mother-State*.

Under Galloway's plan, the government would consist of a grand council whose members would be chosen by the assemblies of each colony. A president-

*Carpenters' Hall, in which the first Continental Congress met. Early on, the Congress still hoped to reach a compromise with the British.*

general, appointed by the king, would have a veto over the acts of the council. The plan, up to that point, might have been acceptable to all the delegates. But when Galloway added that the approval of Parliament would be required for the passage of all acts and laws, many delegates shifted uneasily in their chairs. The plan was narrowly defeated by a vote of 6 to 5. (Rhode Island, which would have made the twelfth vote, lost its say when its delegates split equally on either side of the issue.)

Benjamin Franklin, in England representing the colonies, wrote to Galloway regarding the plan's defeat:

> I have not heard what objections to the plan were made by Congress . . . [but] when I consider the extreme corruption prevalent among all orders of men in this old, rotten state [England], and the glorious public virtue so predominant in our rising country, I cannot but [anticipate] more mischief than benefit from a closer union. . . . I [foresee], therefore, that to unite us intimately will only be to corrupt and poison us also. . . . However I would try any thing, and bear any thing that can be borne with safety to our just liberties, rather than engage in a war . . . unless compelled to it by dire necessity in our own defence.[50]

## The Association

With the defeat of the Galloway plan, the delegates concentrated on the import and export boycott. They had high hopes that the boycott would force England to repeal the Intolerable Acts. On September 29,

*Benjamin Franklin, representing the colonial interests in England, became more and more pessimistic about reaching a compromise between the colonists and the mother country.*

the delegates debated the nuts and bolts of enforcement. The radicals hammered away at one point: Unless the nonimportation principle was strictly upheld in every colony, every port, and every customs house, the proposed boycott would not work. They offered a plan known as the Continental Association, which called for a pledge from all heads of households to neither export nor import goods to or from England.

The Continental Association also called on every county, city, and town to choose inspection committees to enforce the boycott. The committees were to publish the names of all violators of the agreement, so that "all such foes to the rights of British-America may be publicly known,

## "Too Cowardly to Fight"

*Confident of her military superiority, Britain was unconcerned about the colonies' obvious preparations for armed conflict. Historian Page Smith, in* A New Age Now Begins, *discusses British contempt for the colonial soldier.*

"[Britain's] experience in the French and Indian War was that the colonials were poorly trained and unreliable. It was common knowledge, they declared, that the New Englanders would not fight without large quantities of rum. 'Without rum they could neither fight nor say their prayers'; there were 'no meaner whimpering wretches in this universe' than New Englanders sober. United 'by an enthusiastic fit of false patriotism—a fit which necessarily cools in time,' they were nevertheless too cowardly to fight. At the first volley from trained British soldiers, the New Englanders and the Virginians, who were little better, would run for cover to those 'extensive woods which they are too lazy or feeble to cut down.'

The British attitude was colored by class prejudices that held, in effect, that courage was a consequence of good breeding. The common people of every nation [they felt] were, for the most part, cloddish and cowardly. With firm discipline and thorough training, and led by their betters, they could be counted on to give a good account of themselves. But the lower classes (that is to say, in this instance, the colonists), untrained and led by officers very little better than themselves, were hardly to be taken seriously. 'I am satisfied,' wrote Major John Pitcairn, an officer in the Royal Marines, 'that one active campaign, . . . and burning two or three of their towns, will set everything to rights.'"

*The British had little respect for colonial militias from the start. They would pay for their arrogance during the Revolutionary War.*

and universally [scorned] as the enemies of American liberty."[51]

The agreement was signed by all members of Congress, even by Joseph Galloway, who thought it was treasonable. The New Yorker signed, he said, because he considered it to be the only way "of preventing them [the radicals] from proceeding to more violent measures."[52]

The inspection committees—which colonies began appointing as soon as they received the news—attracted many men who had never been active in government, thereby increasing the number of Patriot supporters. By the time the first blood of the Revolution flowed at Lexington, the Continental Association was operating in twelve colonies. Even Georgia, deprived of representation at the Congress, adopted a modified version of the plan.

## Declaration of Rights

Then on October 14, the Continental Congress adopted the Declaration and Resolves. This document conceded that Parliament could regulate commerce (a compromise for the radicals) but rejected as unconstitutional "every idea of taxation, internal or external, for raising a revenue on the subjects in America without their consent."[53] Fundamental rights of the colonists were listed, including life, liberty, and property. British colonists, the declaration contended, were entitled to these rights "by the immutable laws of nature, the principles of the English Constitution, and the several charters or compacts."[54]

The declaration reviewed and condemned the despised Intolerable Acts as "infringements and violations of the rights of the colonists; . . . the repeal of [which] is essentially necessary, in order to restore harmony between Great Britain and the American colonies."[55] The declaration ended with the ominous statement that the colonies were resolved to follow the peaceable methods of economic boycott "for the present only."

Like most of the colonists, the congressional delegates still believed that King George was being deceived by a corrupt Parliament. Accordingly, along with the Declaration of Rights, they submitted a petition to the king, requesting him to right the wrongs Parliament had inflicted.

## First Continental Congress Adjourns

The First Continental Congress adjourned on October 26, 1774. But before adjourning, the body asked Massachusetts to defend themselves only and not to initiate conflict with the royal troops stationed in Boston. In return, Congress promised that if Massachusetts were attacked, the other colonies would come to her aid. The delegates also resolved to meet in six months—again in Philadelphia—if England had not repealed the Intolerable Acts. A date was set for May 10, 1775.

The First Continental Congress was significant because it united the colonies on many issues, not on a single issue as had been the case at the Stamp Act Congress. Technically the Congress was an illegal body; that is, the British government had made it illegal for the colonial assemblies to elect delegates to the meeting in Philadelphia. Some, therefore, have ques-

# An Angry King Writes to His Prime Minister

*King George's bitterness toward the colonies is obvious in this letter to Lord North, written after the First Continental Congress had adjourned. The letter is quoted in* The American Revolution, A Short History *by Richard B. Morris.*

"I returned the private letters received from Lieut. General Gage [royal governor of Massachusetts]; his idea of Suspending the Acts [the Intolerable Acts] appears to me the most absurd that can be suggested; the People are ripe for mischief [and if] the Mother Country [suspends] the measures She has thought necessary this must suggest to the Colonies a fear that alone prompts them to their present violence; we must either master them or totally leave them to themselves and treat them as Aliens; I do not by this mean to [suggest] that I am for [advising] new measures; but I am for Supporting those already undertaken."

*King George was furious at the colonists' demands, which he saw as treasonous.*

tioned its right to pass resolutions. Historians Commager and Morris respond by quoting a writer of that day whose comments about the Continental Congress appeared in the *Essex Gazette:*

> The American Congress derives all its power, wisdom and justice, not from scrawls of parchment signed by kings, but from the people. . . . A freeman in honoring and obeying the Congress honors and obeys himself. The least deviation from the resolves of the Congress will be treason.[56]

A majority of the colonists must have agreed with the Essex writer, because within a few months eleven colonies had approved the actions of the Congress. Only New York, with its large number of Loyalists, withheld ratification. Georgia, not having been represented in the Congress, had no choice either way.

## Outlaw Governments and Minutemen

The colonies had not been idle while the Continental Congress met. Many replaced suspended assemblies with alternative provincial governments. And they prepared to defend themselves. In Concord, after the Powder Alarm, the townsmen had voted

> that there be one or more Companys Raised in this Town by Enlistment and that they Chuse their officers out of

the Body So Inlisted and that Said Company or Companies Stand at a minutes warning in Case of an alarm and when said Company Should be Call[ed] for out of Town, in that Case the Town Pay said Company or Companies Reasonable wages for the time they were absent.[57]

In October the Massachusetts assembly (now a provincial congress), met secretly in Cambridge. They ordered emergency stockpiling of arms and ammunition for the Massachusetts militia's use. A Committee of Public Safety, headed by John Hancock, was authorized to summon the militia if necessary. Appeals went out to all colonies urging that Committees of Safety be established in every town and county. When George Washington returned from the First Continental Congress, he was offered the command of seven of the militia companies in Virginia.

## England Reacts

Meanwhile, in England, the Continental Association was pronounced treasonous. And King George, still believing that only Massachusetts was the problem, declared, "The New England governments are in a state of rebellion, blows [force] must decide whether they are to be subject to this country or independent."[58]

From this point on, colonial newspapers spoke openly of independence. The distant sounds of the drums of war were drawing closer.

# 6 Fighting Begins

After the adjournment of the First Continental Congress in October 1774, events moved swiftly. Local militia units began drilling, and colonists began stockpiling ammunition. All across Massachusetts, Committees of Safety organized selected members of the militia. Called Minutemen, members of this group were to be ready for action on a minute's notice. They also set up a spy network to keep them informed of any movement of the British troops. Massachusetts was prepared to fight, and every day more colonies agreed to back up the New England colony. By mid-1775, Loyalists who openly supported Britain found life in the colonies difficult.

In England, Parliament began 1775 with a debate on what to do about the rebellious Americans. Former prime minister William Pitt, always a supporter of the colonies, called for withdrawal of all troops from Boston. Parliament rejected his motion by a large majority. In February the British legislature approved a petition to the king that declared the colonies in rebellion and called for the use of force to bring them into line once and for all.

*Called Minutemen because they needed to be ready at a moment's notice, men of all ages left their farms and families to join the fight against the British.*

General Gage, commander of the British troops and military governor of Massachusetts since 1774, was ordered to seize the colonial stores of ammunition and arrest troublemakers John Hancock and Sam Adams. But the general had problems. His request for more troops had been denied. And in Boston he was constantly sabotaged and spied upon, unable to make a move without its becoming known. The Patriots had an effective network of spies, among them Paul Revere, who later wrote:

In the fall of '74 and the winter of '75, I was one of upwards of thirty, chiefly mechanics [skilled laborers or craftsmen], who formed ourselves into a committee for the purpose of watching the movements of the British soldiers, and gaining every intelligence of the movements of the Tories. We held our meetings at the Green Dragon. We were so careful that our meetings should be kept secret, that every time we met, every person swore upon the Bible that he would not dis-

## Maryland Exiles a Loyalist

*By mid-1775, Loyalists who openly opposed the Patriots and supported Britain were no longer being tolerated in the colonies. Hezekiah Niles's* Chronicles of the American Revolution *includes a resolution passed by the Maryland Provincial Convention against a Loyalist merchant of Baltimore.*

"Resolved that . . . James Christie, hath manifested a spirit and principle altogether [hostile] to the rights and liberties of America . . . by [opposing] the necessity of introducing a military force into this province, has manifested an inveterate [chronic] enmity to the liberty of this province in particular, and of British America in general.

The said James Christie is and ought to be considered as an enemy to America, and that no person trade, deal, or barter with him hereafter . . . or for the sale or purchase of any part of his real or personal estate, of which he may be at this time seized or possessed.

That [he] be expelled and banished [from] this province forever, and that he depart the province before the first day of September next.

That the said James Christie deposit in the hands of this convention . . . the sum of five hundred pounds sterling, to be expended . . . towards his proportion of all charges and expenses incurred or to be incurred for the defense of America, during the present contest with Great Britain. . . .

That no punishment be inflicted on [him], other than what is now directed by this convention."

cover [divulge] any of our transactions but to Messrs. Hancock, Adams, Doctors Warren, Church, and one or two more. In the winter, towards spring, we frequently took turns, two and two, to watch the soldiers, by patrolling the streets all night.[59]

Nevertheless, General Gage obeyed orders and prepared to seize the gunpowder and supplies that his own spies told him were stored at Concord. If he could also capture Hancock and Sam Adams, so much the better.

## Midnight Message of Paul Revere

Dr. Joseph Warren heard of Gage's plans almost immediately. And on the morning of April 16, 1775, he sent Paul Revere to alert Hancock and Adams, who were hiding out twelve miles northwest of Boston in Lexington. Revere returned to Boston that same night, but on the way he stopped in Charlestown to see Colonel Conant, an active Son of Liberty. Worried that when British troops marched on Concord he might be unable to get out of Boston to warn the countryside, Revere wanted a backup plan. He told Colonel Conant "that if the British went out by water, we would show two lanterns in the North Church Steeple—and if by land one as a signal."[60]

It was not until the night of April 18 that seven hundred royal troops were ferried across Boston Harbor to East Cambridge, where they began the march to Lexington. At the same time, the men and women of Concord were working through

*Paul Revere makes his famous ride. Although he is the rider most people are familiar with, Revere was not the most successful. William Dawes and Samuel Prescott were the two riders who completed their missions, while Revere was captured by British scouts.*

the night to move Patriot arms and ammunition to new hiding places in surrounding towns.

Paul Revere arranged for two lanterns to be hung in the Old North Church. Then he and two friends—expecting shots to ring out at any moment—rowed quietly past the British warship *Somerset* across to Charlestown. Colonel Conant had a horse waiting. Revere rode to Lexington ahead of the Redcoats, spreading the alarm along the way. In Lexington, he awakened Hancock and Sam Adams so they could make their escape. Fleeing across the fields, Adams reportedly said to Hancock, "What a glorious morning this is! I mean for America."[61]

*The Battle of Lexington lasted less than five minutes and left eight colonists dead.*

## First Bloodshed of the American Revolution

The British troops reached Lexington just before sunrise. Captain John Parker and seventy Minutemen waited for them on the Green. Major John Pitcairn, leading a British advance guard of about two hundred men, ordered the Minutemen to lay down their guns. Captain Parker, realizing how badly his men were outnumbered, ordered them to disperse. They began leaving the Green, but still carried their muskets. Major Pitcairn swore at them: "Damn you! Why don't you lay down your arms?"[62]

A shot was fired. It was never established who fired that first shot, but more shots followed immediately as the British fired at the retreating Patriots. Pitcairn tried to restrain his men, but within min-

utes, eight Americans lay dead and ten were wounded. The British soldiers fired a victory volley, shouted a cheer, and continued up the road to Concord, "leaving the citizens of Lexington to gather up their dead and care for the wounded."[63]

## Patriots Fight Back

Paul Revere was captured before he could warn Concord, but other riders got through. Patriots converged on Concord from all directions, even from as far away as Maine and New Hampshire. News of Lexington had spread like wildfire, and no one wanted to be left out of the fight. American forces soon numbered several thousand.

When the British troops arrived in Concord, they sent a platoon of men to

# "Give Me Liberty, or Give Me Death"

*On March 23, 1775, Virginia leaders debated whether Virginia should prepare to fight. Patrick Henry, one of the great orators of the Revolution, spoke. These excerpts from his prophetic speech are from Saul K. Padover's book,* The World of the Founding Fathers.

"This is no time for ceremony. The question . . . is one of [grave importance] to this country. For my own part, I consider it as nothing less than a question of freedom or slavery. . . .

I have but one lamp by which my feet are guided; and that is the lamp of experience. I know of no way of judging of the future but by the past. . . .

I ask gentlemen . . . what means this martial [military] array, if its purpose be not to force us to submission? . . . Has Great Britain any enemy in this quarter of the world, to call for this accumulation of navies and armies? No, sir, she has none. They are meant for us. . . . They are sent over to bind and rivit upon us those chains, which the British ministry have been so long forging. . . . Our petitions have been slighted; our remonstrances [objections] have produced additional violence and insult; our supplications [pleas] have been disregarded; and we have been spurned with contempt from the foot of the throne. . . . There is no retreat. . . . Our chains are forged. Their clanking may be heard on the plains of Boston! The war is inevitable—and let it come!! I repeat it, sir, let it come!!!

Gentlemen may cry, peace, peace—but there is no peace. The war is actually begun! The next gale that sweeps from the north will bring to our ears the clash of . . . arms! . . . Why stand we here idle? . . . Is life so dear, or peace so sweet, as to be purchased at the price of chains and slavery? Forbid it, Almighty God! I know not what course others may take; but as for me, give me liberty, or give me death!"

*Patrick Henry delivers his great speech before the Virginia assembly, concluding with the words that every schoolchild still remembers, "Give me liberty, or give me death."*

guard the North Bridge, while the main body of troops destroyed what little ammunition and supplies they could find. They burned the equipment they found, and the militiamen—seeing the smoke and thinking the village was being burned—began assembling at North Bridge. The British platoon fired on them, killing two men. The Patriots returned the fire, killing three British soldiers and wounding nine. Outnumbered, the British platoon retreated, heading back toward Lexington. They were soon joined in the retreat by their main regiment.

## Bloody Retreat to Boston

The Patriots circled around from North Bridge and waited in the fields along the road, shooting from behind the walls. Using muskets and deer rifles, they kept up a constant barrage of fire at the Redcoats as they passed. The British troops, accustomed to fighting face-to-face and firing as a unit, were helpless against the guerrilla tactics of the colonial sharpshooters. The Redcoats fired aimlessly, wasting their ammunition. General Gage had reinforcements waiting in Lexington, but still the bloody retreat continued.

The Patriots prevented the Redcoats from entering Boston by blocking the Boston Neck, which was the only land entrance into the town. But Colonel Percy, the British regimental commander, managed to march his embattled men over the Charlestown Neck and onto Bunker Hill. There, protected by their warships anchored in the harbor, the exhausted British soldiers waited for boats to carry them across the river to Boston.

British losses had been high, with 73 men killed and 174 wounded. American losses were much lower: 49 killed and 39 wounded. By nightfall on April 19, the British command in Boston no longer doubted whether Americans could or would fight. Colonel Percy wrote to a friend in London:

*Colonists defend North Bridge in Concord. The British expected little resistance when they marched to Concord, but Americans had been forewarned and were prepared to fight.*

*The British hastily retreat from Concord as Patriots shoot at them from all directions during the battle.*

Whoever looks upon them as an irregular mob will be much mistaken. They have men amongst them who know very well what they are about, having been employed as rangers against the Indians. Nor are . . . the men void of a spirit of enthusiasm, for many of them advanced within ten yards to fire at me and other officers though they were . . . certain of being put to death themselves in an instant.[64]

Although the Americans could not prevent British troops from leaving Boston by sea, they could keep the countryside safe from another attack by blocking the Boston Neck. In the meantime, armed men from all over New England continued to arrive. They set up camps outside the city. For a month it was a standoff, with neither side making a move. But during that time, the Second Continental Congress would find the ragtag army a commander in chief.

## Second Continental Congress Meets

On May 10, 1775—still shaken and outraged over the losses at Lexington and Concord—the Second Continental Congress met in the State House in Philadelphia. Many of the delegates had attended the Congress held the preceding year, but there were some new faces. Thomas Jefferson of Virginia, too ill to attend the meeting in 1774, was present. Benjamin Franklin, who had sailed secretly from England in March, arrived in time to serve as a delegate from Pennsylvania. John Hancock, with the sound of British muskets still ringing in his ears, had replaced James Bowdoin in the Massachusetts delegation. Joseph Galloway, the New York conservative turned Loyalist, was not present.

Although the radicals (Patriots) now controlled the Congress, they moved slowly. Only a few members—the Adamses, the Virginians Richard and Arthur Lee, Gadsden of South Carolina, and Franklin—believed that independence was the only answer. But loyalty to the king was still so strong that they hardly dared use the word "independence." Instead they expressed their doubts that any reconciliation was possible.

Two days into their session, the Congress received startling news. Ethan Allen, a Vermont colonial leader, and Captain Benedict Arnold of the Connecticut militia, had led the Green Mountain Boys of Vermont in a surprise attack on the British-held Fort Ticonderoga in upper New York, capturing the fort without firing a shot. Massachusetts had organized this invasion, which clearly was a violation of the "defense only" policy established by the First Continental Congress. But gaining possession of Fort Ticonderoga—even though it would be lost later in the war—proved to be important because the Patriots captured seventy-eight pieces of heavy artillery, including fifty-nine cannons. These were the guns that would finally drive the British out of Boston.

Meanwhile, the standoff around Boston continued. Dr. Joseph Warren, president of the Massachusetts Provincial

## "The Shot Heard Round the World"

*Nineteenth-century poet and essayist Ralph Waldo Emerson wrote "Concord Hymn," read at the dedication of a monument erected to commemorate the battles of Lexington and Concord. The poem, from* The American Tradition in Literature, *vol. 1, edited by Sculley Bradley and others, became Emerson's most famous.*

By the rude bridge that arched the flood,
    Their flag to April's breeze unfurled,
Here once the embattled farmers stood
    And fired the shot heard round the world.

The foe long since in silence slept;
    Alike the conqueror silent sleeps;
And Time the ruined bridge has swept
    Down the dark stream which seaward creeps.

On this green bank, by this soft stream,
    We set to-day a votive stone;
That memory may their deed redeem,
    When, like our sires, our sons are gone.

Spirit, that made those heroes dare
    To die, and leave their children free,
Bid Time and Nature gently spare
    The shaft we raise to them and thee.

*The colonists easily captured Fort Ticonderoga in New York, where only a few British soldiers lived. But getting the seized artillery pieces to Boston proved more difficult.*

Congress, wrote to the Continental Congress requesting the creation of an army under their guidance. "A powerful army on the side of America," Warren wrote, "is the only means left to stem the rapid progress of a tyrannical ministry." [65] And on June 14 Congress agreed to accept the New England militia encamped outside Boston as the Army of the United Colonies. (It would always be called the Continental Army). In addition, rifle companies from Pennsylvania, Virginia, and Maryland were summoned to join the New England militia.

## Washington Appointed Commander in Chief

On the following day Congress resolved that "a General be appointed to command all the continental forces, raised, or to be raised, for the defence of American liberty." [66] The general would receive five hundred dollars a month for pay and expenses. One possible choice was John Hancock, now president of the Continen-

tal Congress. But Hancock was a New Englander. His appointment would not encourage the rest of the colonies to enter the war. John Adams openly lobbied for George Washington, not only because he recognized Washington's gift for leadership, but because the former militia colonel was a Virginian.

On June 14, Adams placed Washington's name in nomination. His nominee, Adams said, was one "whose skill as an officer, whose independent fortune, great talents and universal character [will] command the respect of America and unite the full exertions of the Colonies better than any other person alive." [67]

On June 15, 1775, Washington was unanimously elected commander in chief of the Continental Army. The next day he spoke to the Congress:

> Mr. President, Tho' I am truly sensible of the high Honour done me in this Appointment, yet I feel great distress from a consciousness that my abilities and Military experience may not be equal to the extensive and important Trust: However, as the Congress de-

*What Washington lacked in military experience, he gained in popularity with his troops. Here he passes among his soldiers.*

sires I will enter upon the momentous duty, and exert every power I Possess In their Service for the Support of the glorious Cause. . . .

As to pay, Sir, I beg leave to Assure the Congress that as no pecuniary [financial] consideration could have tempted me to have accepted this Arduous [very demanding] employment I do not wish to make any profit from it: I will keep an exact Account of my expences . . . and that is all [the pay] I desire.[68]

Within a week General Washington set off for Boston to assume his command. Along the way he learned of the Battle of Bunker Hill that had been fought on June 17.

## Battle of Bunker Hill

General Gage had received reinforcements that brought the number of British troops in Boston up to ten thousand, not counting the sailors and marines. The colonial militiamen encamped around Boston numbered about five thousand. They learned through their spies that the British planned to take possession of Bunker Hill as a first step toward occupying Dorchester Heights, a strategic point in Boston. To prevent this, on the night of June 16 the Patriots sent sixteen hundred militiamen to fortify Bunker Hill. After a long discussion, they decided to build their main fortification on Breed's Hill, which was closer to Boston. Only secondary fortifications were erected on Bunker Hill. This was a major tactical error, since Breed's Hill was the smaller hill, and therefore more vulnerable.

Next morning, seeing the forts, the British attacked. The Patriots, led by Colonel William Prescott, were badly outnumbered. Nevertheless, the British detachment of twenty-six hundred men had to make three charges up the hill before the Patriots were forced to retreat. On each charge, Colonel Prescott ordered his men not to fire until the British were only a few steps away. The Redcoats fell in devastating numbers—fifty at a time from one single round of fire.

Although the British finally captured Bunker Hill, it was a costly victory. Their losses were crushing—226 killed and 828 wounded, most of whom would die later. The Patriot losses, which occurred mostly during the retreat, numbered 140 killed and 271 wounded. It was in one sense a victory for the Americans because it removed any awe they had felt for the formidable British army. General Gage wrote home, "Those people shew a spirit and conduct against us, they never shewed against the French."[69]

When the battle ended, John Pitcairn, the British major who had led the attack at Lexington, lay dead. Also killed was the Patriot Dr. Joseph Warren, who had sent Paul Revere on his midnight ride. Abigail Adams wrote to her husband, John, in Philadelphia:

> Not all the havoc and devastation they have made has wounded me like the death of Warren. We want him in the Senate; we want him in his profession; we want him in the field. We mourn for the citizen, the senator, the physician, and the warrior. May we have others raised up in his room.[70]

In the meantime, the congressional delegates were in the uncomfortable position of trying to go two different ways at once. Reluctant to take the final step and declare independence, they continued to do everything in the name of the king. At the same time, they prepared to protect themselves against the king's armies. This internal conflict caused Congress to make contradictory decisions.

Even as Washington took command of the Continental Army in Boston, the Continental Congress made one final attempt to reconcile with England. The so-called Olive Branch Petition was drafted by John Dickenson who, although he remained a Patriot, had grown more moderate. The appeal to the king read in part:

> We solemnly assure your Majesty, that we not only most ardently desire the former harmony between [Britain] and these colonies may be restored, but that a concord [peace] may be established between them upon so firm a basis, as to perpetuate its blessings uninterrupted by any future dissentions to succeeding generations in both countries.[71]

*At Bunker Hill, the British defeated the colonists when the fight became one of hand-to-hand combat, but they paid a heavy price.*

John Adams angrily protested the Olive Branch Petition, claiming it showed weakness. He wrote in a letter to a friend that Dickenson had given "a silly cast to our whole doings."[72]

## "Bring the Traitors to Justice"

On August 23, 1775, George III issued a proclamation that the colonists were in "open and avowed rebellion" and that every attempt should be made "to suppress such rebellion and to bring the traitors to justice."[73] Two days later, the Olive Branch Petition arrived from the colonies. The king refused to consider it.

These events forced the colonists to look at the king in a different light. They had always viewed the king favorably, seeing him as a victim of an unscrupulous Parliament. He had been the one link with England they were anxious and willing to preserve. By proclaiming the colonists rebels and refusing to hear their appeals, the king strengthened the arguments of those who advocated independence.

Then on December 22, Parliament destroyed any chance of reconciliation by closing all American ports to trade. This meant that American ships and their cargoes could be seized by the Royal Navy, "as if [they] were open enemies."[74]

By this time, ten of the thirteen colonies had established their own independent governments. The "governments" were run by the suspended assembly members who now called themselves provincial congresses. Many royal governors had fled to the safety of British warships. Still the colonists held back from declaring independence. Their ambivalence was demonstrated by the official American flag, being flown by General Washington on a hill near Boston and by the ships of the newly formed American navy. The flag had thirteen stripes that represented the unity of the colonies, but it also displayed the British Union Jack, to symbolize unity with Great Britain.

Clearly, neither radicals nor conservatives found it easy to sever all ties with the mother country. But the colonies would soon have to make a decision. They could not "forever remain half in, half out of the empire, professing allegiance while refusing obedience."[75]

*America's first official flag bore a striking resemblance to the British Union Jack.*

# 7 The Spirit of 'Seventy-Six

Colonial Americans greeted the year 1776 with both sadness and anger. The majority had always assumed that their demands would be met and that they would remain a part of the British Empire. But they were rapidly losing their sentimental view of England as the mother country. The king had refused to help them and had now declared all the members of the Continental Congress traitors. That declaration had led many of the undecided in Congress to support independence, since they knew that if they were caught they would be hanged, no matter which stand they had taken. Across the colonies, the word "independence," though mostly unspoken, was in the air.

## "Tis Time to Part"

Yet, even as the Patriots engaged in active fighting against the king's troops and forced royal governors to flee to England, they still did not make the break. A catalyst was needed. It came in the unlikely person of Thomas Paine, an Englishman who had been in the colonies for only a year, a man who had failed at everything he'd ever tried to do.

Thomas Paine's pamphlet *Common Sense* was published on January 10, 1776.

Within three months, the forty-seven-page booklet sold 120,000 copies. Passed from hand to hand, it was read by at least half of the people in the thirteen colonies, who then read it to others. Before Paine, most political tracts were written for the well educated. *Common Sense* was written in language that the common person could understand.

Paine ridiculed the divine right of kings: "Of more worth is one honest man to society and in the sight of God, than all the crowned ruffians that ever lived."[76] Knowing he risked being hanged, he became the first person openly to attack King George, whom he identified as the "Royal Brute of Britain."[77] Most important, though, was his clear call for independence—publicly stating what many colonists were beginning to feel, but had not yet put into words. "Everything that is right or natural," he wrote, "pleads for separation. The blood of the slain, the weeping voice of nature cries, 'TIS TIME TO PART.'"[78]

Paine did not call for overthrowing George III and replacing him with another monarch. He advocated a republic, government in which the people, through their elected representatives, would have supreme power. Historian Edmund Morgan says of Paine, "At one stroke he pro-

## COMMON SENSE;

ADDRESSED TO THE

## INHABITANTS

OF

## AMERICA,

On the following interesting

## SUBJECTS.

I. Of the Origin and Design of Government in general, with concise Remarks on the English Constitution.

II. Of Monarchy and Hereditary Succession.

III. Thoughts on the present State of American Affairs.

IV. Of the present Ability of America, with some miscellaneous Reflections.

Man knows no Master save creating HEAVEN,
Or those whom choice and common good ordain.
THOMSON.

PHILADELPHIA;
Printed, and Sold, by R. BELL, in Third-Street.

MDCCLXXVI.

*Thomas Paine's pamphlet* Common Sense *was a bestseller by colonial standards. Paine's eloquent defense for an independent and democratic United States rallied many colonists to support the Revolution.*

pelled Americans into the great discovery of human equality toward which they had been moving unwittingly ever since they first denied Parliament's right to tax."[79]

Even George Washington was impressed by *Common Sense*, declaring shortly after its publication: "The pamphlet *Common Sense*, will not leave numbers at a loss to decide upon the propriety [properness] of a separation."[80] It was Washington's first public statement favoring independence.

In late January, King George made it easier for the colonists to consider independence. He signed a treaty with Germany that sent twenty thousand hired soldiers to the colonies. The soldiers, or mercenaries, were called Hessians because many of them were from the German state of Hesse-Cassel. They had a reputation as cruel and barbaric fighters. Outraged that the king would dispatch such an army against his subjects, many who had opposed independence changed their minds. And in Cambridge, General Washington, not yet concerned with Hessians, concentrated on the Redcoats in Boston and on his own woefully inadequate army.

## Creating an Army

When George Washington took command of the new Continental Army, it was composed only of militiamen. Shocked by their unprofessional manner, the future president surveyed his undisciplined, unorganized, untrained troops and wrote: "Could I have foreseen what I have, & am [likely] to experience, no consideration upon Earth should have induced me to accept this command."[81]

The Continental Army would always be a combination of militiamen and men recruited especially for it, called Continentals or regulars. The militiamen fought bravely, but they lacked discipline. They were part-time soldiers, whose only obligation was to their states. As such they were unreliable, sometimes leaving in the middle of a battle because their enlistment time was up. Enlistments ranged from a few weeks to a few months. Washington was himself relatively inexperienced, but he was not a man who backed away from a challenge. He set to work establishing a regular army. He urged men to enlist for at least one year, and he worked to bring about order through discipline and organization.

## British Leave Boston

Early in 1776, the Redcoats, still recovering from their losses at Bunker Hill, waited quietly in Boston for reinforcements from England. This gave Washington some much-needed time. Even so, he lacked the necessary artillery to force the British out of Boston and was glad to receive help from an unexpected source.

Washington had appointed as chief of artillery a colonel named Henry Knox, who had no battlefield experience. Prior to his appointment, however, Knox, a 280-pound bookseller, had studied book after book on

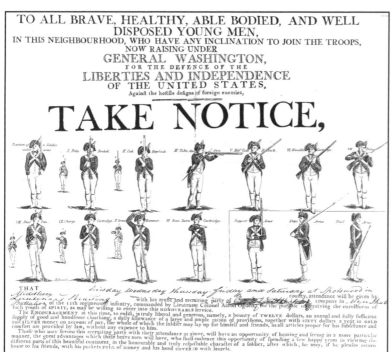

*(Above) A Continental soldier. Although inexperienced, the average Continental soldier was enthusiastic, patriotic, and believed deeply in his cause. (Left) Recruiting notices similar to this asked all able-bodied men to enlist in the Continental Army.*

military tactics, had drilled with the Boston militia, and had carefully observed the maneuvers of the Redcoats stationed in Boston. Now he suggested bringing to Boston, by sled, the artillery captured the preceding year at Fort Ticonderoga.

## Fortifying Dorchester Heights

Colonel Knox, who had left Washington's camp in Massachusetts in November 1775, was back in Cambridge by the end of January 1776 with fifty cannons. He had supervised the moving of the heavy artillery across three hundred miles of snow-covered mountains. It was one of the most remarkable feats of the war.

During the night of March 4, 1776, Washington's men dragged the cannons to the top of Dorchester Heights, overlooking Boston Harbor and the British ships anchored there. The next morning General William Howe—who had replaced General Gage as the British commander—seeing the fortified hill, realized that his troops could no longer hold Boston, since American guns were aimed at them. Failure to fortify Dorchester Heights had been a major British blunder.

As Washington watched, Howe's men began loading arms, supplies, and equipment onto their ships. Although they left in haste, the Redcoats took time to plunder the houses and stores of Boston. On March 17, General Howe and his nine thousand troops sailed away. Eleven hundred Loyalists, who dared not remain in Boston without British protection, left with them. It was Washington's first victory, but it was not yet time to celebrate. British troops from Ireland and Canada were already attacking the South.

*Using barges and sleds, Colonel Knox and his men haul heavy artillery over three hundred miles from Fort Ticonderoga in New York to General Washington in Boston.*

*General Howe and his nine thousand troops sail out of Boston Harbor after General Washington's first victory.*

Although there had been no formal declaration of war, and no American declaration of independence, the British military had devised a plan to force the rebellious colonists into submission. They divided the colonies into three main arenas of war: the New England colonies, the Middle colonies, and the Southern colonies.

Convinced that most southerners were Loyalists, the British attacked first in that region. They expected to quell the rebellion there quickly, restore royal government, establish a military base in North Carolina, and move on to the next arena.

However, when North Carolina Loyalists attacked the Patriot militia at Moore's Creek Bridge near Wilmington on February 27, 1776, they suffered a crushing defeat. British troops, learning of the disaster, abandoned plans to land in North Carolina. Instead they headed for Charleston, South Carolina, only to be driven off by local Patriots, who damaged British ships and inflicted over two hundred casualties. Following that humiliating defeat, the British sailed for New York. They had not only failed to establish a Southern base, they had strengthened the South's commitment to independence.

Meanwhile in Philadelphia, John Adams, Franklin, Jefferson, and other delegates to the Second Continental Congress continued to argue for independence.

## Independence at Last

By spring of 1776, thanks to Paine's *Common Sense* and Washington's bloodless victory in Boston, public sentiment increasingly turned toward independence. In Philadelphia, John Adams wrote, "By every Post [mail delivery] and every day, Independence rolls in on us like a torrent."[82] In April the Continental Congress ordered American ports opened to all countries except England. And in May it encouraged the individual colonies to establish their own governments. Colony after colony began instructing delegates to

## "A Wonderful Production"

*The response to Thomas Paine's* Common Sense *echoed through the colonies. Newspapers printed and reprinted it along with their own reactions. This excerpt from an editorial in the* Constitutional Gazette *originally appeared February 27, 1776. It was reprinted in Frank Moore's* Diary of the Revolution.

"The pamphlet entitled 'Common Sense,' is indeed a wonderful production. . . . The author introduces a new system of politics, as widely different from the old, as the Copernican system [of astronomy, in which the earth revolves around the sun] is from the Ptolemaic [in which the earth is the center of the universe]. The blood wantonly spilt by the British troops at Lexington, gave birth to this extraordinary performance, which contains as surprising a discovery in politics as the works of Sir Isaac Newton do in philosophy [physics]. This animated piece dispels, with irresistible energy, the prejudice of the mind against the doctrine of independence, and pours in upon it such an inundation [overflowing] of light and truth, as will produce an instantaneous and marvellous change in the temper—in the views and feelings of an American. The . . . delight with which it is [read] . . . is a demonstration that the seeds of independence, though imported with the troops from Britain, will grow surprisingly with proper cultivation in the fields of America. The mind indeed exults at the thought of a final separation from Great Britain . . . and although the ties of affection . . . have formerly bound this country . . . to Great Britain, yet the connexion will be dissolved. . . . 'For the blood of the slain, the voice of weeping nature cries it is time to part.'"

vote for independence. Then, on May 15, the Virginia Convention (the old House of Burgesses) voted to instruct its delegates to introduce a motion for independence to the Congress.

On Friday, June 7, Virginia delegate Richard Henry Lee, who had long argued for independence, rose in Congress to propose a resolution. It was an electric moment. All the delegates knew what was coming. Fifty men leaned forward in their chairs as Lee began to read from the paper in his hand:

RESOLVED: That these United Colonies are, and of right ought to be, Independent States, that they are absolved from all allegiance to the

(Below) The five-man drafting committee works on the Declaration of Independence. From left to right are Benjamin Franklin, Thomas Jefferson, John Adams, Robert Livingston, and Roger Sherman. (Above) The document is signed on July 4, 1776.

British Crown, and that all political connection between them and the State of Great Britain is, and ought to be, totally dissolved.[83]

Congressional moderates, with a last show of strength, managed to postpone voting on the resolution, but a committee was appointed to draw up a formal declaration of independence. The committee chose one of its members, Thomas Jefferson, to write the first draft.

On July 1, Congress debated Richard Henry Lee's motion. When the vote was taken, it was 9 to 4 for independence—not a clear enough majority for such an important decision.

That night the radicals worked furiously to change the minds of dissenting delegates. Caesar Rodney, whose Delaware

## Boston After the British

*These reminiscences of a Bostonian, describing Boston after the departure of the British, were printed in the* Boston Cential. *Hezekiah Niles included them in his* Chronicles of the American Revolution.

"On passing into the town, it presented an indescribable scene of desolation and gloominess, for notwithstanding the joyous occasion of having driven our enemies from our land, our minds were impressed with an awful sadness at the sight of the ruins of many houses which had been taken down for fuel . . . the wretched appearance of the very few inhabitants who [had] remained during the siege—the contrast between the Sunday we then beheld, compared with those we formerly witnessed, when well dressed people, with cheerful countenances, were going to, and returning from church . . . but more especially when we entered the Old South church, and [saw] that it had been turned into a *riding school*, for the use of general [John] Burgoyne's regiment of cavalry. . . . The pulpit and all the pews were taken away and burnt for fuel, and many hundred loads of dirt and gravel were carted in, and spread upon the floor. The south door was closed, and a bar was fixed, over which the cavalry were taught to leap their horses at full speed. A grog shop was erected in the gallery, where liquor was sold to the soldiery, and consequently produced scenes of riot and debauchery in that holy temple. All these circumstances conspired to fill the mind with somber reflections. But amidst the sadness of the scene, there was a pleasing satisfaction in the hope that men capable of such atrocities, could not have the blessing of Heaven in their nefarious [vicious] plan of subjugating our beloved country."

delegation had voted against independence, rode all night (eighty miles) through a raging thunderstorm to reach Philadelphia in time to swing Delaware's vote to a vote for independence.

On July 2, the delegates voted again. Twelve colonies voted for independence. New York, with its large population of Loyalists, abstained. John Adams wrote to his wife: "Yesterday the greatest question was decided which ever was debated in America, and a greater, perhaps, never was nor will be decided among men."[84]

Congress, now the acting government, turned its attention to Jefferson's draft of the Declaration of Independence.

## The United States of America

On July 4, 1776, Congress, after some amendments and deletions, adopted Jefferson's draft of the Declaration of Independence. The document has two parts. The first part, the preamble, justifies any people's right to overthrow a government that denies them their natural rights. The preamble, which reflects the influence of John Locke, states:

> We hold these truths to be self-evident, that all men are created equal, that they are endowed by their Creator with certain unalienable Rights, that among these are Life, Liberty, and the Pursuit of Happiness.[85]

The Pulitzer Prize–winning historian Samuel Eliot Morison says of this preamble:

> These words are more revolutionary than anything written by [French revolutionary Maximilien] Robespierre, [radical German political philosopher Karl] Marx, or [Russian revolutionary leader V. I.] Lenin, more explosive than the atom, a continual challenge to ourselves as well as an inspiration to the oppressed of all the world.[86]

The second part of the declaration lists colonial grievances against the king. Jefferson was the first to officially use the title of "United States of America" when he concluded the declaration:

> WE, THEREFORE, the Representatives of the UNITED STATES OF AMERICA . . . in the Name, and by Authority of the good People of these Colonies . . . are . . . Absolved from all Allegiance to the British Crown.

*It was done.* With the adoption of the Declaration of Independence, the British colonists in America became Americans. The thirteen colonies became thirteen united states. But their work had just begun. Now they had to become a nation, not just on paper but in reality.

## Second Continental Congress Governs

The new country had no national government. This was a difficult problem, because the people were reluctant to grant power to a central government for fear of ending up with another tyranny. On the other hand, political leaders understood the need for a central power of some kind. England had always directed commerce, foreign policy, and defense in the colonies. A national government was needed to take over that role. Congress appointed a committee to draft a plan of unity, or confederation.

The plan, called the Articles of Confederation and considered to be the first U.S. constitution, advocated a much stronger national government than Congress was willing to accept. After the issues had been debated, a compromise was reached.

The Articles provided for a federal system of government but gave the most important powers, including control of the money, to the states. Congress could ask for money, but the states could refuse to supply it. Congress could make decisions, but the states could vote them down. Congress could declare war and make treaties, but it could not raise an army, levy taxes, or enforce its own laws.

However, the Articles were not ratified by the states until March 1781. Consequently, the United States fought most of the war with no more government than an informal agreement among the states that allowed Congress to direct the war and handle foreign affairs.

The lack of a true national government caused problems for Washington and his army. Congress had to rely on the often reluctant states to provide money to pay soldiers and supply the army with food, clothing, weapons, and equipment. Washington spent the war training new armies. It was difficult to convince men to reenlist when they were seldom paid, often had little or nothing to eat, and lacked proper clothing. Much of the war was fought on promises. Soldiers were promised free land, and the five thousand black soldiers who fought for the Patriot cause were promised freedom. Despite the hardships and frustrations, and although it came close to being destroyed in 1776, the Continental Army survived, in great part because of Washington's leadership.

## "Times That Try Men's Souls"

When General Howe and his troops left Boston in March 1776, Washington was certain Howe would attempt to occupy New York City: "It is the Place that we must use every Endeavor to keep from them," he wrote. "For should they get that Town . . . they can stop [communication] between the northern and southern Colonies, upon which depends the Safety of America."[87]

In April, Washington marched his troops from Boston to New York. Arriving ahead of the British, he divided his army between Brooklyn Heights and Manhattan. General Howe landed on Staten Island in July. His brother, Admiral Richard Howe, arrived with the British fleet a few days later. These land and sea forces, combined with the Hessian troops, totaled forty-five thousand experienced soldiers and sailors.

Washington, with only twenty thousand men, was unable to hold Brooklyn Heights. He retreated to Manhattan where, in September, General Howe again attacked. Forced once again to retreat, Washington and his troops fled to New Jersey, leaving New York City in the hands of the British. It would remain so until the end of the war.

Howe chased Washington's army across New Jersey toward the Delaware River. By December the Continental Army was near total collapse. They had known nothing but defeat and retreat, and morale was low. "These are the times that try men's souls," Thomas Paine wrote in *The Crisis.*[88]

Surprisingly, General Howe failed to pursue his advantage. After forcing Washington across the Delaware River into Pennsylvania, Howe ended his campaign for the winter, sending most of his soldiers back to New York. As far as Howe was concerned, the campaign of 1776 was over.

## A Crucial American Victory

Washington, however, had other ideas. He knew that in Trenton, New Jersey, there was a brigade of Hessian soldiers that might, at any time, attack Philadelphia. (The members of the Continental Con-

*Washington and his troops attempt to cross the Delaware River into New Jersey in a surprise attack on British troops.*

gress had already fled to Baltimore for safety.) He also knew that the six-month enlistments of half his already depleted army would be up in January. With a record of nothing but devastating defeats along with the hardships Continental soldiers endured, it would be difficult, if not impossible, to get reenlistments. In a daring move, Washington planned a surprise attack against the Hessians.

On the memorable night of December 25, 1776, Washington, with twenty-five hundred men—some without shoes, many without warm coats—recrossed the Delaware in a blinding snowstorm. The crossing was treacherous because of swift currents and ice chunks that clogged the river. They surprised the sleeping Hessians, killing or wounding over a hundred and taking a thousand prisoners. No Americans were killed. An American soldier gave a mocking summary of the battle: "Hessian population of Trenton at 8 A.M.,—1,408 men and 39 officers; Hessian population 9 A.M.,—0."[89]

The victory lifted the spirits of all Americans—both civilians and soldiers. Enlistments picked up. However, the war was far from over. Some of the darkest days were still ahead.

# Chapter

# 8 War and Peace

The British approached the 1777 military campaign with a blueprint for victory. They planned to use their Canadian force, led by General Burgoyne, to gain control of the Hudson River valley, completing the cutting off of New England from the rest of the colonies. They could then concentrate on the south. Their strategy called for Burgoyne to lead an army south from Canada to Albany, New York. He would be joined from the west by another Canadian detachment led by Lieutenant Colonel Barry St. Leger. At the same time General Howe, already occupying New York City, prepared to capture Philadelphia.

In September, Howe and Washington met at the Battle of Brandywine Creek near Philadelphia. Washington, badly outnumbered, tried to block Howe from entering the capital city, but was forced to retreat. By September 26, British troops occupied Philadelphia. Washington retaliated on October 4, attacking Howe's army camped at Germantown (north of Philadelphia). Although the Americans were defeated, their near victory prevented Howe from joining Burgoyne. Howe settled down for the winter in Philadelphia, while Washington and his dwindling army retired to nearby Valley Forge.

## Victory at Saratoga

Meanwhile, General Burgoyne had started out well by recapturing Fort Ticonderoga—the fort that had provided the guns to drive the British from Boston. But then his campaign went awry. St. Leger was attacked by Benedict Arnold and forced to retreat to Canada. Harassed by

*British general Burgoyne surrendered his entire army to American general Horatio Gates on October 17, 1777. Burgoyne would later write to his wife, "If Old England is not by this lesson taught humility, then she is an obstinate old slut, bent upon her ruin."*

*The Battle of Saratoga proved to be a critical turning point in the war for the Americans. The American victory proved that the colonists could viably fight the British and allowed Benjamin Franklin to convince France to enter the war in favor of the colonies.*

the Green Mountain Boys of Vermont, bogged down by officers' wives and children plus thirty horse-drawn carts of the general's personal luggage, Burgoyne's army made slow progress.

The American northern army, led by General Horatio Gates, met Burgoyne at Saratoga, New York. Burgoyne attacked twice, but each time he was forced back, mostly because of the fierce and heroic leadership of Benedict Arnold. "Nothing," wrote Captain Wakefield of the Continental Army, "could exceed the bravery of Arnold on this day."[90]

On October 17, 1777, Burgoyne surrendered his entire army of some fifty-seven hundred men. As the top commander, Gates took credit for the victory, refusing to acknowledge Arnold's help. Arnold, who had already been passed over for promotions he deserved, began to wonder whether England might appreciate him more.

The loss of Burgoyne's army hardly affected the large supply of soldiers available to England, but it helped Benjamin Franklin convince France to enter the war. For that reason, the victory at Saratoga was a turning point in the Revolution.

## Franklin in France

The Continental Congress had sent Benjamin Franklin to France in November 1776—five months after adoption of the Declaration of Independence. Franklin's reputation preceded him. He was the most famous American abroad. He spoke flawless French, and his work on electricity had been published all over Europe.

France had been waiting since the French and Indian War in 1763 for revenge against the English. Franklin's task was to convince the French government that the Revolutionary War offered them that opportunity. He spent eighteen months patiently making friends. The comte de Vergennes, foreign minister for Louis XVI, was the first to yield to Franklin's influence. King Louis was more reluctant. But with news of the American victory at Saratoga, Franklin sent a message to Vergennes, saying:

We have the Honour to acquaint your Excellency that we have just receiv'd an Express from Boston . . . with [news] of the total Reduction of the

*Benjamin Franklin patiently and ardently courted French officials in his efforts to get their support for the Revolution. The French were captivated by Franklin's lack of airs and his authentic manner.*

Force under General Burgoyne, himself & his whole Army having surrendered themselves Prisoners.[91]

Two days later, Louis XVI responded that he was ready to talk to the American representatives.

The Saratoga victory also disturbed British officials. They offered to meet all colonial demands "short of open and avowed independence."[92] Once again it was too little, too late. By now the Americans would accept nothing less than full independence.

Not wanting a last-minute reconciliation between England and her former colonies, France was now eager to join in an alliance with America. However, because France and Spain had an agreement to act together in any decisions that might lead to war, France needed Spain's approval.

Spain had been cooperating with France in providing supplies to America. But fearing that his own colonies might follow America's example, King Charles III had refused to form an alliance with the revolutionaries. The French, owing to the skillful manipulation of Franklin, who kept them thinking that England and

America might reconcile any day, decided to act without Spain.

In February 1778, France and America signed two treaties. One regulated trade between the two countries. The other was a treaty of alliance in which both agreed that if either was in a war, the other would rush to the rescue. This was, in effect, a declaration of war by France against England, and marked the first time America was recognized as an independent nation.

Spain entered the war the next year, but as an ally of France, not of America. However, the results were the same. With both France and Spain in the war, England had to fight on several fronts. Large numbers of troops and ships that would have been sent to America had to be kept in England to guard against possible invasion. The American war for independence became a world war.

## Continental Army Suffers at Valley Forge

While Franklin charmed and pressured the French, Washington and his army struggled to survive the winter at Valley Forge. The first two months were the worst. The soldiers, living in tents, half-naked and close to starving, rushed to get huts built before the harshest weather set in. Colonel John Brooks of Massachusetts wrote to a friend on January 5, 1778:

> For a week past we have had snow, and as cold weather as I almost ever knew at home. To see our poor brave fellows living in tents, bare-footed, bare-legged, bare-breeched, etc. etc., in snow, in rain, on marches, in camp, and on duty, without being able to supply their wants is really distressing.[93]

By mid-February, the men had finished building their huts. Although they were still without winter clothes, they had plenty of wood for their fireplaces. Food became more plentiful as foraging parties scoured the countryside for edible plants and animals. The parties also seized food from suspected Loyalist supporters. A spirit of

*Washington's troops spend a bitter winter at Valley Forge.*

camaraderie prevailed among the soldiers. They pooled their clothes, so that a soldier forced to go out into the cold could have a complete outfit. "Washington and those men who remained with him that winter," writes Page Smith, "formed a bond of unity that could never be broken."[94]

The Continental Army would also emerge from Valley Forge much improved in fighting skills, thanks to one man, a foreigner.

## Drill and Discipline

Baron Friedrich von Steuben, formerly a staff officer under Frederick the Great of Prussia, joined Washington at Valley Forge. This was fortunate, because one of Washington's major problems was lack of a standard manual of arms. And his independent colonial soldiers were not accustomed to prompt obedience.

Happily, drilling soldiers was Steuben's specialty. He drew up a manual of arms, and formed and drilled a model company of soldiers. Within a few weeks the men Steuben had been working with looked so sharp that the whole camp became drill-conscious. The Prussian officer was a cheerful person who instilled pride in the men. He also understood the American soldier, and he passed along this analysis to a European friend:

> The genius of this nation is not in the least to be compared with the Prusians, the Austrians or French. You say to your soldier, "Do this," and he doeth it, but I am obliged to say, "This is the reason that you ought to do that," and then he does it.[95]

*Baron Friedrich von Steuben, pictured here at Valley Forge, was a master at precision drills. Steuben is credited with drilling members of the Continental Army until they were able to listen and respond to verbal commands.*

At Washington's suggestion, Steuben was appointed inspector general of the Continental Army. The Americans were ready for the spring campaign.

## A New and Improved Continental Army

At the same time, the British were making their own preparations. In May 1778, they replaced General Howe with Sir Henry Clinton. The new commander was ordered to abandon Philadelphia, move to New York, and devise a strategy for attacking the south.

As Clinton's army moved toward New York, Washington followed closely, waiting for an opportunity to attack. His chance came on June 28 at Monmouth Courthouse in New Jersey. Against his better judgment, Washington allowed General Charles Lee, a brilliant but eccentric former British soldier, to lead the attack.

*Although the Battle of Monmouth ended in a draw, it was considered a victory for Washington (shown upon his horse), who merely needed to prove that the Continental Army was a force to be reckoned with.*

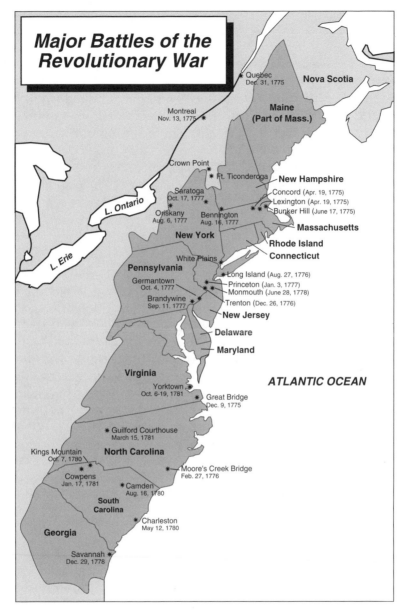

## Major Battles of the Revolutionary War

Quebec
Dec. 31, 1775

Nova Scotia

Montreal
Nov. 13, 1775

Maine
(Part of Mass.)

Crown Point

Ft. Ticonderoga

New Hampshire

Saratoga
Oct. 17, 1777

Concord (Apr. 19, 1775)
Lexington (Apr. 19, 1775)
Bunker Hill (June 17, 1775)

Oriskany
Aug. 6, 1777

Bennington
Aug. 16, 1777

L. Ontario

Massachusetts

New York

Rhode Island
Connecticut

L. Erie

White Plains

Long Island (Aug. 27, 1776)

Pennsylvania

Germantown
Oct. 4, 1777

Princeton (Jan. 3, 1777)
Monmouth (June 28, 1778)

Brandywine
Sep. 11, 1777

Trenton (Dec. 26, 1776)

New Jersey

Delaware

Maryland

Virginia

ATLANTIC OCEAN

Yorktown
Oct. 6-19, 1781

Great Bridge
Dec. 9, 1775

Guilford Courthouse
March 15, 1781

Kings Mountain
Oct. 7, 1780

North Carolina

Cowpens
Jan. 17, 1781

Moore's Creek Bridge
Feb. 27, 1776

Camden
Aug. 16, 1780

South
Carolina

Georgia

Charleston
May 12, 1780

Savannah
Dec. 29, 1778

On the day of the battle, Lee disregarded orders, and his leadership was incompetent almost to the point of treason. An angry George Washington, seeing Lee's troops in complete disarray, some retreating, some fighting, brushed Lee aside, and took charge himself. A young French nobleman, the marquis de Lafayette, who would have led the attack had it not been for Lee's seniority, later wrote about Washington on that day:

General Washington seemed to arrest fortune with one glance. . . . His presence stopped the retreat. . . . His graceful bearing on horseback, his

## General Washington Discouraged

*Five months before the war-ending victory at Yorktown, Washington experienced his lowest period of the war. France had not sent the promised naval support, and the American states had failed to supply the required number of men. Washington's May 1, 1781, diary entry, which reflects his discouragement, is quoted in Samuel Eliot Morison's* The Oxford History of the American People.

"Instead of having [storehouses] filled with provisions, we have a scanty pittance scattered here and there in the different States. Instead of having our arsenals well supplied with military stores, they are poorly provided, and the workmen all leaving them. Instead of having the various articles of field [equipment] in readiness to deliver, the Quartermaster General . . . is but now applying to the several States to provide these things for the troops. . . . Instead of having a regular system of transportation . . . all that business, or a great part of it, [is] being done by military impress [force]. We are daily and hourly oppressing the people—souring their tempers—and alienating the affections. Instead of having the regiments compleated . . . which ought to have been [done] by the 1st of February . . . scarce any State in the Union has, at this hour, an eighth part of its quota [of men] in the field and little prospect, that I can see, of ever getting more than half. In a word—instead of having everything in readiness to take the field, we have nothing; and instead of having the prospect of a glorious offensive campaign before us, we have a bewildered and gloomy defensive one—unless we should receive a powerful aid of ships, land troops, and money from our generous allies [France and Spain]; and these, at present, are too [unpredictable] to build upon."

calm and deportment which still retained a trace of displeasure [anger at Lee] . . . were all calculated to inspire the highest degree of enthusiasm. . . . I thought then as now that I had never beheld so superb a man.[96]

The British retreated. During the night they broke camp and slipped away. Clinton's army reached New York City safely, but the Battle of Monmouth had introduced the British to a new Continental Army.

Washington positioned his troops in a land blockade around New York City. He hoped for the arrival of French troops to end the standoff. But three years would pass before the alliance with France bore fruit.

During the remainder of 1778 and much of 1779, the war consisted primarily of hit-and-run raids by each side. This changed when the war shifted from the north to the south.

## The War Moves South

Clinton sent forces to Georgia and by the end of December 1779, Savannah, and soon the entire state, was in British hands. Meanwhile Clinton, accompanied by another general, Lord Cornwallis, as second in command, sailed from New York with a fleet of ninety ships carrying eighty-five hundred troops. His objective was Charleston, South Carolina.

Washington sent many soldiers to help hold Charleston, but finally the city was cut off. On May 12, 1780, after a month's siege, Charleston surrendered. The Americans lost their entire southern army—fifty-four hundred men. A jubilant Clinton returned to the north, leaving his men under the command of Cornwallis.

The Americans hastily assembled a second southern army of regulars and militia. Over Washington's protests, Congress appointed General Gates as commander. Gates, heavily outnumbered, launched a direct attack against Cornwallis at Camden, South Carolina, on August 16, 1780. Compounding that mistake, Gates put militiamen in charge of a key area of his line. When the British charged, with drums beating and bayonets flashing, these untrained men panicked. Officers tried to calm the terrified men, but they "ran like a torrent," flowing past the officers "and . . . spread through the woods in every direction."[97] The regular soldiers continued to fight against overwhelming odds, and mostly without leadership after their commanding general also fled. Ortho Williams, an American colonel present at Camden, wrote:

> If in this affair the militia fled too soon, the regulars may be thought almost as blamable for remaining too long on the field, especially after all hope of victory must have been despaired of. . . . The officers of the brigades . . . never received orders to retreat, nor any order from any *general* officer. The brave Major General, the Baron de Kalb, fought on foot . . . and fell mortally wounded into the hands of the enemy . . . a fate which probably was avoided by other generals only by an opportune retreat.[98]

Colonel Williams, in his reference to "other generals," is undoubtedly referring to commanding general Gates, who was almost as quick to flee as the frightened militiamen. Gates's flight was one of the most shameful episodes of the war for the Americans, and it ended the man's military career.

Alexander Hamilton, Washington's aid and secretary, wrote to James Duane, a member of the Continental Congress:

> Was there ever an instance of a general running away, as Gates has done, from his whole army? And was there ever so [hasty] a flight? One hundred and eighty miles in three days and a half. It does admirable credit to the activity of a man at his time of life. But it disgraces the general and the soldier. . . . What will be done by Congress? Will he be changed [replaced] or not? If he is changed, for God's sake . . . send Greene.[99]

The disaster at Camden—with an estimated thousand Americans killed or wounded—marked the lowest point in the war for the revolutionaries. In a period of four months, the British had captured two American armies and controlled the mid-Atlantic coast from Georgia to North Carolina. To add to Washington's woes, word came the day after the Camden defeat that the American commander's most capable general, Benedict Arnold, defected to the British. It would have been difficult on that dark day to convince either Washington or the country that the tide was soon to turn.

## Americans Fight Back

But following the Battle of Camden, Congress allowed Washington to choose a new general to replace Gates. In October 1780 he appointed Nathanael Greene. It was a good choice. The thirty-eight-year-old Greene knew the region, and he, like Washington, recognized the kind of war that had to be fought. He used hit-and-run tactics to harass the British. Cornwallis, who to this point had seemed undefeatable, could win only half-victories against Greene. And Greene always inflicted more losses than his own army sustained. "We rise," Greene said, "get beat, rise, and fight again."[100]

In March 1781, at the Battle of Guilford Courthouse in North Carolina, Cornwallis forced Greene to retreat, but British casualties numbered five hundred. Cornwallis wrote to General William Phillips in Virginia, "If we mean an offensive war in America, we must abandon New York and bring our whole force into Virginia."[101] Clinton, the commanding general, refused to leave New York, but he gave Cornwallis permission to march north into Virginia.

## Victory at Yorktown

During that spring and summer of 1781, American troops led by Steuben and Lafayette, forced Cornwallis and his army to the coast in Yorktown, Virginia. Lafayette reported Cornwallis's position to Washington, who—along with a French army under comte de Rochambeau—was still blockading Clinton in New York.

In August, Washington learned that the long-promised French naval support was on the way. Comte de Grasse was sailing from the West Indies with a large French fleet bound for Chesapeake Bay outside Yorktown. Washington made plans to move all available French and American land forces to join Lafayette at Yorktown.

On September 5, Admiral de Grasse and his fleet attacked and disabled the British navy in Chesapeake Bay. The siege of Yorktown began on September 28 with Washington in full command. The allied French and American soldiers steadily closed in on Cornwallis, bombarding his forts and inflicting casualties. Cornwallis was trapped. The British navy could not help him, and his ammunition and food supplies were running out. On October 19, 1781, at 2:00 P.M., his army of more than eight thousand soldiers surrendered, as the British band played a marching song called "The World Turned Upside Down."

The victory at Yorktown effectively ended the hostilities. Officially the war would not be over for two more years, but Yorktown was the last major battle. The

## America, That Jewel

*William Cowper, one of England's outstanding poets and essayists during the revolutionary period wrote about the war to his friend John Newton, a British clergyman. This excerpt from a letter written on March 30, 1783, five months before the peace treaty was signed, is in a selection of the poet's correspondence edited by E. V. Lucas.*

"The powers of Europe have clashed with each other to a fine purpose; that the Americans, at length declared independent, may keep themselves so, if they can; and that what the parties . . . have wrested from each other in the course of the conflict may be . . . restored to the proper owner. . . . England . . . has in some instances acted with a spirit of cruel animosity she [could not have been accused of] till now. . . . On the other hand, the Americans, who, if they had contented themselves with a struggle for lawful liberty, would have deserved applause, seem to me to have incurred the guilt of parricide [killing a close relation], by renouncing their parent, by making her ruin their . . . [objective], and by associating themselves with [England's] worst enemy [France], for the accomplishment of their purpose. France, and of course Spain, have acted a treacherous, a thievish part. They have stolen America from England, and whether they are able to possess themselves of that jewel or not hereafter, it was doubtless what they intended. . . . [England] is the only injured party. America may, perhaps, call her the aggressor; but if she were so, America has not only repelled the injury, but done a greater."

event was not a military disaster for England, however. The eight thousand captured British soldiers, after all, represented only about a quarter of the British forces in the New World. And the British navy was still intact. The importance of Yorktown was the effect it had on the British government.

When news of the defeat reached England, Lord North, the prime minister, faced a full-scale rebellion in the House of Commons. On first hearing about Yorktown, North exclaimed, "Oh, God! It is all over."[102] He resigned from his position of leadership on March 20, 1782. The new government was committed to peace.

## A Separate Peace

Lord Shelburne, England's new prime minister, sent an ambassador to Paris to begin peace talks. He was Richard Oswald, a millionaire Scottish merchant who had spent his youth in Virginia. To represent the United States, the Continental Congress appointed Franklin, who was already in Paris; John Adams, who was in Holland negotiating a peace treaty; and John Jay, who had been serving as the American diplomat in Spain. The men were instructed to demand recognition of American independence, but Congress also ordered them to act only with the knowledge and agreement of France in their negotiations. John Jay, by nature suspicious, was unwilling to follow these instructions.

Jay knew that because neither Spain nor France wanted a strong republic in North America, the European powers were determined to see that America gained as little as possible from England. The future chief justice discovered, as well, a secret treaty in which France had promised to Spain the return of Gibraltar (an English possession) and possibly title to new territory—a portion of Georgia and the Mississippi Valley. Both Jay and Adams felt this arrangement justified them in ignoring congressional instructions and negotiating a separate peace with England. Franklin, at first reluctant, eventually agreed that it would best serve the new nation's interest to negotiate with the British in secrecy.

The terms of the final peace treaty, called the Treaty of Paris, were amazingly favorable to the United States. The treaty fully recognized American independence, and Britain promised to withdraw all troops as soon as possible. The boundaries of the new country were established: The United States was to consist of all land between the Atlantic Coast and the Mississippi River and between the Great Lakes and the Florida border. The United States, for its part, agreed to pay all debts owed to England, pledged not to persecute the Loyalists, and said it would allow people who had fled the colonies to return.

England offered the generous peace terms because an agreement with America would free British troops still in New York City and Charleston to attack the French in the West Indies. Thus the threat of a separate peace with America could be used to force a general peace with France and Spain.

The Treaty of Paris was signed on September 3, 1782, but it was not ratified by all parties until April 17, 1783. Only then did Franklin feel confident enough to write Charles Thomson, secretary of the Continental Congress: "Thus the great and hazardous enterprise we have been engaged in, is, God be praised, happily completed; an event I hardly expected I should live to see."[103]

# 9 "A New Scene Opens"

The Revolutionary War ended in 1783 with the ratification of the peace treaty. But the difficult task of building a strong and united government lay ahead. In August 1782, Alexander Hamilton—a young New Yorker who would play an important role in the new government—had written to his friend John Laurens:

> Peace made, my dear friend, a new scene opens. The object will be to make our independence a blessing. To do this we must secure our Union on solid foundations—a herculean [mighty] task. . . . It requires all the virtue and all the abilities of our country.[104]

The states had become more unified during the war when they were joined together in a common effort. But in peacetime, they went back to warring over boundary lines—even charging each other import and export taxes. Once again, the loyalty of most Americans was to their own state. The Continental Congress became a debating arena for bitter state disagreements.

To make matters worse, the country suffered a severe economic depression after the war. As colonies, Americans had operated within a worldwide British trading network. As independent American states, those trade outlets were closed to them. In historian Darrett Rutman's words, they "found themselves thrust out of the parental home and forced to find their own way in the world."[105] Each of the states owed war debts and had war damage. And no help could be expected from the powerless national government. Consequently, the states continued to print worthless paper money, which destroyed their credit. Then, to restore credit, they imposed heavy taxes—taxes the people had no money to pay.

## Nationalists Come Onstage

Under these conditions, people across the country grew more and more rebellious. It became increasingly obvious that government under the Articles of Confederation was not working. Changes were needed to establish a balance between national and state governments. In 1786, with mob violence increasing, George Washington wrote to John Jay: "We have errors to correct. We have probably had too good an opinion of human nature in forming our Confederation."[106]

Leaders like Washington—Nationalists who favored a strong central government—had long supported the idea of a constitutional convention to revise and amend the Articles of Confederation. Their opponents, who favored a weak central government and strong state governments, had always prevented such a convention.

But the Nationalists persisted. They were convinced that the United States could never be a strong nation without a powerful central government. They presented their arguments in newspapers and pamphlets, and they exchanged ideas with one another. Nothing happened until January 21, 1786, when James Madison, a member of Congress and an outspoken Nationalist, made a proposal to the Virginia state legislature. He called for a national convention to discuss the country's economic crisis and the possibility of amending the Articles of Confederation.

## The Annapolis Convention

Responding to Madison's suggestion, Virginia invited all the states to a convention at Annapolis, Maryland, in September. Three ardent Nationalists who attended— Madison from Virginia, Hamilton from New York, and Dickenson from Pennsylvania—saw the conference as their last opportunity to save the country. Time was short because the Continental Congress was already seriously discussing breaking the nation into three separate republics.

But only five states sent delegates to Annapolis. Such a small group could only talk, because any amendment to the Articles of Confederation required agreement of all thirteen states. Those who did attend agreed that the economic ills of the country were connected to the weaknesses

*Congressman James Madison called for a national convention to discuss the country's future after the Revolutionary War. Many colonists opposed the formation of a strong national government.*

of the national government. Upon adjournment, they sent a report, not only to the legislatures of the five participating states, but also to the executives of the other states and to the Congress. In their report they called for another convention

> to advance the interests of the union . . . to meet at Philadelphia on the second Monday in May next [year], . . . to devise such further provisions as shall appear to them necessary to render the constitution of the Federal Government adequate to the exigencies [urgent needs] of the Union.[107]

Many like John Jay, who supported a powerful central government, believed that such a convention would have no legal or constitutional standing unless it was called by the Confederation Congress. Thus the Nationalists waited anxiously for the legislature's reaction to their report. Finally in February 1787, Congress reluctantly agreed to issue a call to the states for the Philadelphia convention. They em-

---

## "The Revolution Is Not Over"

*Dr. Benjamin Rush, Philadelphia physician, statesman, and author, spoke to all Americans in a speech in 1787 just prior to the opening of the Constitutional Convention. This excerpt is from Hezekiah Niles's* Chronicles of the American Revolution.

"There is nothing more common, than to [confuse] the terms of the American revolution with those of the late American war. The American war is over; but this is far from being the case with [the] American revolution. On the contrary, nothing but the first act of the great drama is closed. It remains yet to establish and perfect our new forms of government. . . .

It is often said, 'that the sovereign and all other power is seated in the people.' This idea is unhappily expressed. It should be—'all power is derived from the people,' they possess it only on the days of their elections. After this, it is the property of their rulers; nor can they . . . resume it, unless it be abused.

The people of America have mistaken the meaning of the word sovereignty; hence each state pretends to be sovereign. . . . No individual state, as such, has any claim to independence. She is independent only in a union with her sister states in congress.

I am extremely sorry to find a passion for retirement so universal among the patriots and heroes of the war. . . . Patriots of 1774, 1775, 1776—heroes of 1778, 1779, 1780! come forward! your country demands your services! Philosophers and friends to mankind, come forward! your country demands your studies and speculations! Lovers of peace and order, who declined taking part in the late war, come forward! your country forgives your timidity and demands your influence and advice! Hear her proclaiming, in sighs and groans, in her governments, in her finances, in her trade, in her manufactures, in her morals, and in her manners, 'The Revolution Is Not Over!'"

phasized, however, that it was "for the sole and express purpose of revising the Articles of Confederation and reporting to Congress and the several legislatures such alterations.[108] Nothing was mentioned about replacing the Articles.

Both Madison and Hamilton doubted that the convention would ever take place. They knew that because the states feared strengthening the national government, any suggestion to amend the Articles would meet with strong resistance. And at first their doubts appeared to be justified. Only Pennsylvania was quick to elect delegates to a convention that probably was not going to meet. Then a new development changed the country's thinking.

## Shays's Rebellion

Even before the Annapolis meeting, the desperate Massachusetts farmers—crushed by high taxes, afraid of losing their farms, and tired of petitioning a legislature that ignored them—had taken the law into their own hands. Armed citizens, trying to hold off any further judgments of debt, had prevented county courts from convening.

Daniel Shays, against his will, had become the leader of the rebellious citizens. Shays, who had served with distinction as a captain in a Massachusetts regiment, had returned from the war expecting finally to be paid for his military service. Like the other veterans, he was still waiting. On January 26, 1787, Shays led a raid on the federal arsenal in Springfield, but the Massachusetts militia quickly subdued his small group, and the rebellion was over.

However, news of the uprising in Massachusetts had a great influence on public opinion. It was frightening to realize that the national government had been powerless to help Massachusetts. Moreover, uprisings accompanied by civil disobedience had occurred in more than half the states. In this crisis atmosphere amid a fear of mob rule and anarchy, the states began electing delegates to the Philadelphia convention. By March it was clear that at least nine states would send delegates.

## Preparing for Philadelphia

During the winter of 1787, Nationalists prepared for the convention. Because the word "Nationalist" was distressing to the many Americans who still feared a strong national government, the supporters of this philosophy began to call themselves Federalists. This forced their opponents— those who favored strong states' rights and a weak federal government—to call themselves Anti-Federalists.

The goal of the Federalists was to write a new constitution to replace the old one— the Articles of Confederation. This could have been interpreted as illegal, since Congress had not given the convention such authority. For that reason, Madison, the acknowledged leader of the Nationalists, realized that Washington and Franklin must be present: the awe-inspiring Washington to give the convention respectability, and the eighty-one-year-old Franklin, one of the most famous people in the world, to give it credibility and legitimacy.

Aware that Washington was reluctant to come out of retirement, Madison corresponded regularly with his fellow Virgin-

## Preamble to the Constitution

*The preamble to the Constitution, written by Gouverneur Morris, designates the people as the government's source of authority.*

"We the People of the United States, in Order to form a more perfect Union, establish Justice, insure domestic Tranquility, provide for the common defence, promote the general Welfare, and secure the Blessings of Liberty to ourselves and our Posterity, do ordain and establish this Constitution for the United States of America."

---

ian. He described, with enthusiasm, his ideas for the new constitution and kept Washington up to date on the election of delegates to the convention. In April, just a month before the scheduled convention, Madison wrote to Jefferson in France: "Pennsylvania has added Dr. Franklin to her [delegation]. There is some ground to calculate on the attendance of General Washington."[109] Later Madison would write Jefferson:

> To forsake the honorable retreat to which [Washington] had retired and risk the reputation he had so deservedly acquired, manifested a zeal for the public interest that could, after so many and illustrious services, scarcely have been expected of him.[110]

Throughout the winter, Madison—using Jefferson's library—made notes on the history of government. He wrote a series of memos detailing what was wrong with all existing governments including the Confederation.

If, in the words of the American poet Joel Barlow, "the revolution [was] but half completed,"[111] then Madison set out for Philadelphia well prepared to finish it.

## "An Assembly of Demi-Gods"

The Constitutional Convention opened in Philadelphia on May 25, 1787. Fifty-five delegates assembled in the State House. Jefferson, with some justification, called the delegates "an assembly of demi-gods."[112] Out of this assembled group would come two presidents, two chief justices, and six future state governors. Almost every delegate had served in a colonial or state legislature. Eight had signed the Declaration of Independence. And at least thirty had served in the Revolutionary War.

Absent were John Adams, Thomas Jefferson, and John Jay, all of whom were in Europe on government missions. Also missing were many of the radicals of 1776. Richard Henry Lee (who had proposed the Declaration of Independence) and Patrick Henry, both elected delegates, refused to come—as did most Anti-Federalist leaders, who resisted a strong national government. Some, as in the case of Sam Adams, did not attend because they had not been elected.

The delegates present were, for the most part, a new generation. They had not

*Washington presided over the Constitutional Convention with unanimous approval.*

played a major role in the struggle for independence. They respected the ideas and attitudes of that era, but they saw a desperate need to restructure them to fit the problems of the 1780s. Unlike the radicals in 1776, their goal was "the creation, not the destruction, of national power."[113]

The majority of the delegates, whether Federalists or Anti-Federalists, wanted a stronger federal government. On the other hand, they did not want to lose the rights they had gained from the Revolution. The problem of balancing the two would be the convention's main topic of debate.

## Gentlemen, You May Start the Debate

The convention opened with Washington's unanimous election as president of the convention. Edmund Randolph, a Vir-ginia delegate, immediately proposed fifteen resolutions called the Virginia Plan. It could just as accurately have been called the Madison Plan, since Madison had written it.

It was soon clear that the Virginia Plan went far beyond the convention's stated purpose to amend the Articles of Confederation. Instead, it proposed the creation of a three-part government to administer the law-making, executive, and court functions of the nation. The first part, or branch, would consist of a two-house, or bicameral, national legislature. The lower house would be elected by the people. The upper house would be picked by the lower house from candidates elected by state legislatures. The number of representatives in both houses would be based on state populations. The second part, a president or national executive, with veto power over congressional acts, was to be chosen by Congress. The third branch of the three-part government was to be a separate and independent judicial system, headed by a Supreme Court.

The Virginia Plan, in effect, moved to discard the Articles of Confederation, uniting the states under a strong national government. Washington, who had watched his army starve and freeze because of a weak central government, thoroughly approved of this plan.

The smaller states, however, were concerned that if representatives of the lower house were elected by the people, the small states would always be outvoted. And if

## Franklin on the Constitution

*It seems fitting that Benjamin Franklin, the oldest of the nation's founders, was the last to comment on the proposed constitution before the convention adjourned on September 17, 1787. This excerpt is from Saul K. Padover's* The World of the Founding Fathers.

"I confess that I do not entirely approve of this Constitution at present; but . . . I am not sure I shall never approve it; for, having lived long, I have experienced many instances of being obliged, by better information or fuller consideration, to change my opinions even on important subjects, which I once thought right, but found to be otherwise.

I agree to this Constitution, with all its faults—if they are such; because I think a general Government necessary for us, and there is no *form* of government but what may be a blessing to the people, if well administered; and I believe . . . that this is likely to be well administered for a course of years, and can only end in despotism [tyranny], as other forms have done before it, when the people shall become so corrupted as to need despotic government, being incapable of any other. I doubt, too, whether any other Convention we can obtain, may be able to make a better constitution; for, when you assemble a number of men, to have the advantage of their joint wisdom, you inevitably assemble with those men all their prejudices, their passions, their errors of opinions, their local interests, and their selfish views. It therefore astonishes me . . . to find this system approaching so near to perfection as it does; and I think it will astonish our enemies, who are waiting with confidence to hear . . . that our States are on the point of separation. . . . Thus I consent . . . to this Constitution, because I expect no better, and because I am not sure that it is not the best."

seats were apportioned according to population, they would again be in the minority.

Consequently, William Paterson of New Jersey, leading the small states, offered an alternative called the New Jersey Plan. This plan proposed one vote for each state. It basically did little more than amend the Articles of Confederation, although it gave Congress much-needed authority in two areas: taxation and trade. Under the New Jersey Plan, Congress would have the powers to tax and to regulate both foreign and interstate commerce.

After three days of intense debate, the New Jersey Plan was defeated by a vote of 7 to 3, with two states not voting and a third state's vote canceled by a split in its delegation. The defeat virtually guaranteed that the convention would discard the Articles of Confederation and set up a central government. But fierce debating had caused many of the more moderate Federalists to waver. They began questioning whether the Virginia Plan went too far. States' rights, they realized, must not be ignored.

## Compromises, Great and Small

Clearly, if the goal of a strong national government was to be achieved, compromises would be necessary. "The extraordinary feature of the Philadelphia convention," writes Darrett Rutman, "was that the delegates could surmount their fears and prejudices, hammering out one practical compromise after another in the interest of 'a more perfect union.'"[114]

From the middle of June to the beginning of August, the convention moved through the individual parts of the Virginia Plan. The most controversial point was deciding how the separate states, big and small, should be represented in Congress. Should representation be proportional to population? Delegates from the small states were adamant. No, it should not. The small states would be swallowed up and exploited by the large states. Ridiculous, the large-state delegates argued; the small states had nothing to fear.

The weather was hot, and the delegates' tempers were hotter. Arguments grew ugly, turning into shouting matches. Small-state delegates hinted at forming foreign alliances if they were refused equality of representation. Large-state delegates hinted that they might be forced to take up arms against the small states to prevent the formation of such alliances.

At this point, Benjamin Franklin proposed a compromise. He used the following comparison in suggesting the appointment of a separate committee to consider the question of representation:

> When a broad table is to be made, and the edges of the planks do not fit, the artist takes a little from both, and makes a good joint. In like manner here both sides must part with some of their demands, in order that they may join in some accommodating proposition.[115]

A committee was formed that included one member from every state. Out of this committee came the Great Compromise: The states were given equal representation in the upper house, the Senate (which pleased the small states), and representation by population in the lower chamber, the House of Representatives (which pleased the large states). None of the delegates was totally happy with the compromise, but most accepted it.

The question of how slaves—who were not considered to be citizens—should be counted in a state's population was also settled in this compromise. Counting the slaves as individuals would have given the states in which slavery was widely practiced a far higher representation in Congress. It was decided that five slaves would be counted the same as three free white men.

Many delegates opposed the whole idea of slavery. And through their efforts, a ban on the slave trade after 1808 was included (in Article I, Section 9). In the interest of drafting a constitution that would be accepted by the people, however, the complete elimination of the institution of slavery in the United States had to be left for future generations.

## Final Touches

By the end of July, the convention chose a Committee of Detail to write a rough draft of the constitution. It took them ten days. The delegates then spent from August 6 to September 10 debating and refining the draft, clause by clause. After the content had been approved, they turned the document over to a Committee of Style, made up of the convention's most talented writers. One of those, Gouverneur Morris, a Pennsylvania delegate, was responsible for the superb language of the preamble. Unlike the Articles of Confederation, which always spoke to the states, the preamble establishes the connection of the Constitution to the people, in its opening lines: "We the People of the United States . . ."

Of the fifty-five delegates who had convened in May, thirty-nine signed the finished Constitution on September 17. Some had left early on, either in disgust or in anger. Others had hung on through the sizzling Philadelphia summer, but in the end refused to sign. Neither the Federalists nor the Anti-Federalists were completely happy with the final product. And perhaps, like Franklin, most felt that they could "expect no better." But the wise old Pennsylvanian's overall outlook was positive, for he concluded by saying "and . . . I am not sure that it is not the best." [116]

## The Final Battle

Those who signed the Constitution knew that getting it ratified by the states would be difficult. After the convention adjourned, Washington wrote to Lafayette that the Constitution "is now a child of fortune, to be fostered by some and buffeted by others." [117]

The convention had already overstepped its legal bounds by creating a replacement for the Articles of Confederation. Now the members went further and insisted that the Constitution be submitted directly to the people for approval, rather than to state legislatures. Ratification was to be obtained in specially elected state conventions whose delegates had been elected by the people. Knowing that it was unrealistic to expect approval from all thirteen states, the framers had specified in Article VII that ratification by only nine states would be sufficient to make the proposed constitution law. Congress debated for ten days before sending the document to the state legislators, who then began calling for ratifying conventions.

As soon as the Constitutional Convention adjourned on September 17, the Federalists began working on the problem of ratification. On October 27, 1787, the first of eighty-five articles, that would later be collected and published as the *Federalist*, appeared in New York City newspapers. These articles were written by Alexander Hamilton, James Madison, and John Jay under the pen name of Publius. The *Federalist* was influential in achieving ratification and continues to be used as an authoritative commentary on the Constitution.

In the state conventions, the battles that had been fought in Philadelphia had to be fought all over again. The Federalists, who supported the Constitution, had the backing of Franklin and Washington. But above all, they offered positive solutions. The Anti-Federalists could only oppose the material submitted. They had nothing new or better to suggest. However, they could point out—as did Jefferson, a Federalist supporter—that the Constitution as submitted contained no language to protect the natural rights of individuals from governmental abuse of power. The Federalists argued that such

*The Constitution of the United States, perhaps the most significant and enduring document in history.*

## Jefferson Wants Bill of Rights

*Thomas Jefferson, on assignment in France, kept himself informed of the convention's proceedings and offered his opinions. Following is an excerpt from a letter written to James Madison on December 20, 1787, after the convention had adjourned. It appears in Padover's book,* The World of the Founding Fathers.

"I like much the general idea of framing a government, which should go on of itself, peaceably, without . . . [continually turning] to the State legislatures. I like the organization of the government into legislative, judiciary and executive. I like the power given the legislature to levy taxes, and for that reason solely, I approve of the [larger] House [House of Representatives] being chosen by the people directly. . . . I am captivated by the compromise of the opposite claims of the [big] and little States. . . . There are other good things of less [importance, but] I will now tell you what I do not like. First, the omission of a bill of rights, providing clearly . . . for freedom of religion, freedom of the press, protection against standing armies, restriction of monopolies, the eternal and unremitting force of the habeas corpus laws [laws against illegal imprisonment], and trials by jury in all matters . . . triable by the laws of the land. . . . A bill of rights is what the people are entitled to against every government on earth, general or particular; and what no just government should refuse, or rest on inference.

It is my principle that the will of the majority should prevail. If they approve the proposed constitution in all its parts, I shall concur in it cheerfully, in hopes they will amend it, whenever they shall find it works wrong."

protection was implied because the national government was limited to certain powers. But, as the Anti-Federalists reminded them, that was what England had said. Madison then promised that the first business of the new government would be to enact a "bill of rights," which would list the desired assurances.

On June 26, 1788, New Hampshire became the ninth state to ratify. Congress declared the Constitution law, and selected March 4, 1789, as the date for the new government to begin.

On February 4, 1789, George Washington, by unanimous choice, became the first president of the United States of America. On September 25, the new Congress passed into law the first ten amendments to the Constitution, which together make up the Bill of Rights. Dr. Benjamin Rush, the Pennsylvania Federalist, wrote: "Tis done. We have become a nation."[118]

# Legacy of Hope

The American Revolution, as John Adams pointed out, "was in the minds of the people."[119] The enterprising men and women who survived the hardships of early colonization in America refused to tolerate any interference in local affairs. These colonial Americans were determined to control their own destiny. And from Lexington and Concord to Valley Forge and Yorktown, they never lost sight of that goal.

The legacies of 1776 are not limited to the United States of America. Thomas Jefferson's Declaration of Independence proclaimed the rights not just of Americans, but of all people. It expressed the new and radical idea that governments were created to serve the people and had no right to act without the people's consent. The American Revolution launched a worldwide struggle for equality and created a new respect for human rights. The willingness of a handful of courageous British colonists to fight for government by the people—in a world dominated by kings—inspired citizens everywhere to rise up in defense of individual liberty and freedom.

The eighteenth century was a cruel age, characterized by tyrannical governments that oppressed and exploited the people. When thirteen quarrelsome colonies succeeded in establishing a free republic, others were encouraged to break free from oppression. The French Revolution, the revolutions in South and Central America, and the Russian Revolution all had their roots in 1776.

*A commemorative painting published in 1876 entitled "'76." The American Revolution would give hope and encouragement to peoples of other nations to rise up against their governments.*

*A poster commemorates the Bill of Rights. The struggle to maintain the rights of the people, with liberty and justice for all, continues on a daily basis.*

In 1861 Abraham Lincoln declared that the principle embodied in the Declaration of Independence was not the mere matter of the separation of the colonies from the mother land; but something in that Declaration giving liberty, not alone to the people of [America], but hope to the world for all future time.[120]

Thomas Jefferson reverently labeled America's founders "demi-gods," but in truth they were mortals bound by the limitations of their own era. They had to balance idealism with the realities of their time. Nevertheless, they created a constitution that has survived—with few changes—for over two hundred years. Today, the principles of that document continue to protect American liberties. Whenever freedoms are at risk, Americans turn to the Constitution and the Bill of Rights.

The American Revolution made possible a continuing quest for civil liberty and social justice. But America has not yet reached the idealistic goals envisioned by its founders. Some U.S. citizens still struggle for their "unalienable Rights." The American Revolution did not end in Paris with the signing of the peace treaty. It did not end in Philadelphia with the signing of the Constitution. The Revolution will never end as long as Americans struggle to create a free and a just society.

# Notes

### Introduction: Inheritance of Liberty

1.   Quoted in Richard B. Morris, *The American Revolution, A Short History*. 1955. Reprint, New York: Krieger, 1979, p. 89.

2.   Bernard Bailyn, *The Ideological Origins of the American Revolution*. Cambridge, MA: The Belknap Press of Harvard University Press, 1967, p. 66.

3.   Thomas Jefferson, *The Declaration of Independence: The Evolution of the Text as Shown in Facsimiles of Various Drafts by Its Author, Thomas Jefferson*. Edited by Julian P. Boyd. Princeton, NJ: Princeton University Press, 1945, p.2.

4.   Quoted in Larry R. Gerlach, ed., *Legacies of the American Revolution*. Logan: Utah State University, 1978, p. 15.

### Chapter 1: Old World to New World

5.   Quoted in Henry Steele Commager and Richard B. Morris, eds., *The Spirit of 'Seventy-Six, The Story of the American Revolution as Told by Participants*. 1958. Reprint, New York: Harper & Row, 1967, p. 302.

6.   Quoted in Page Smith, *A New Age Now Begins*, vol. 1. New York: McGraw-Hill, 1976, p. 182.

7.   Quoted in Darrett B. Rutman, *The Morning of America 1603–1789*. Boston: Houghton Mifflin, 1971, p. 41.

8.   Quoted in Gary B. Nash and Julie Roy Jeffrey et al., eds., *The American People, Creating a Nation and a Society*. New York: Harper & Row, 1986, p. 33.

9.   Quoted in Ola Elizabeth Winslow, ed., *Harper's Literary Museum, Early American Writings*. New York: Harper & Brothers, 1927, p. 16.

10.   Rutman, *The Morning of America*, pp. 110–11.

11.   Quoted in L. H. Butterfield, ed., *Diary and Autobiography of John Adams*, vol. 2. Cambridge, MA: The Belknap Press of Harvard University Press, 1961, p. 109.

12.   Quoted in Rutman, *The Morning of America*, pp. 96–97.

13.   Smith, *A New Age Now Begins*, vol. 1, p. 59.

14.   Quoted in Bailyn, *The Ideological Origins of the American Revolution*, p. 168.

### Chapter 2: Colonial America by 1763

15.   Quoted in Richard M. Ketchum, *The World of George Washington*. New York: American Heritage, 1974, p. 35.

16.   Rutman, *The Morning of America*, p. 148.

17.   Rutman, *The Morning of America*, p. 148.

18.   Quoted in Winslow, *Harper's Literary Museum, Early American Writings*, p. 380.

19.   Quoted in Saul K. Padover, ed., *The World of the Founding Fathers*. 1960. Reprint, Cranbury, NJ: Barnes, 1977, p. 149.

20.   Bailyn, *The Ideological Origins of the American Revolution*, p. 47.

21.   Quoted in Bailyn, *The Ideological Origins of the American Revolution*, p. 3.

22.   Quoted in Ronald William Clark, *Benjamin Franklin: A Biography*. New York: Random House, 1983, p. 159.

23.   Quoted in Clark, *Benjamin Franklin*, p. 159.

### Chapter 3: England Steps Up Its Control

24.   Quoted in Martin Kallich and Andrew MacLeish, eds., *The American Revolution Through British Eyes*. New York: Harper & Row, 1962, p. 3.

25. Quoted in Merrill Jensen, *The Founding of a Nation, A History of the American Revolution 1763–1776*. New York: Oxford University Press, 1968, p. 84.

26. Quoted in Bernard Bailyn, *Faces of the Revolution*. New York: Knopf, 1990, p. 140.

27. Quoted in Robert Middlekauff, *The Glorious Cause, The American Revolution, 1763–1789*. New York: Oxford University Press, 1982, pp. 74, 75.

28. Quoted in Hezekiah Niles, *Chronicles of the American Revolution*. Edited by Alden T. Vaughan. New York: Grosset & Dunlap, 1965, p. 11.

29. Quoted in Frank N. Magill, ed., *Great Events from History* (American Series), vol. 1. 1907. Reprint, Englewood Cliffs, NJ: Salem Press, 1975, p. 221.

30. Quoted in Edmund S. Morgan, *The Birth of the Republic, 1763–89*, 15th ed. Chicago: University of Chicago Press, 1969, p. 32.

31. Quoted in Kallich and MacLeish, *The American Revolution Through British Eyes*, p. 31.

### Chapter 4: Propelled Toward Revolution

32. Quoted in Smith, *A New Age Now Begins*, vol. 1, p. 319.

33. Quoted in Catherine Drinker Bowen, *John Adams and the American Revolution*. 1949. Reprint, Boston: Little, Brown, 1950, pp. 396–97.

34. Quoted in Esmond Wright, *Fabric of Freedom, 1763–1800*. 1961. Reprint, New York: Hill and Wang (division of Farrar, Straus and Giroux), 1964, p. 67.

35. Quoted in Esther Forbes, *Paul Revere and the World He Lived In*. 1942. Reprint, New York: Book-of-the-Month Club, 1983, p. 182.

36. Quoted in Forbes, *Paul Revere and the World He Lived In*, p. 189.

37. Smith, *A New Age Now Begins*, vol. 1, p. 384.

38. Quoted in Commager and Morris, *The Spirit of 'Seventy-Six*, p. 10.

39. Quoted in Samuel Eliot Morison and Henry Steele Commager, *The Growth of the American Republic*, vol. 1, 5th ed. New York: Oxford University Press, 1962, p. 176.

40. Quoted in Commager and Morris, *The Spirit of 'Seventy-Six*, p. 12.

41. Quoted in Commager and Morris, *The Spirit of 'Seventy-Six*, p. 18.

### Chapter 5: Colonies Begin to Unite

42. Quoted in Commager and Morris, *The Spirit of 'Seventy-Six*, p. 39.

43. Quoted in Wright, *Fabric of Freedom*, p. 88.

44. Quoted in Jack N. Rakove, *The Beginnings of National Politics, An Interpretive History of the Continental Congress*. New York: Knopf, 1979, p. 45.

45. Quoted in Butterfield, *Diary and Autobiography of John Adams*, vol. 2, p. 120.

46. Quoted in Smith, *A New Age Now Begins*, vol. 1, p. 431.

47. Quoted in Commager and Morris, eds., *The Spirit of 'Seventy-Six*, p. 54.

48. Quoted in Butterfield, *Diary and Autobiography of John Adams*, vol. 2, pp. 134, 135.

49. Quoted in Samuel Eliot Morison, *The Oxford History of the American People*, vol. 1. 1965. Reprint, New York: Penguin Books, 1972, p. 278.

50. Quoted in Samuel Eliot Morison, ed., *Sources and Documents Illustrating the American Revolution, 1764–1788, and the Formation of the Federal Constitution*, 2nd ed. Oxford: Oxford University Press, 1961, p. 137.

51. Quoted in Morison, *Sources and Documents Illustrating the American Revolution*, p. 124.

52. Quoted in Morris, *The American Revolution*, p. 47.

53. Quoted in Morison, *Sources and Documents Illustrating the American Revolution*, p. 120.

54. Quoted in Morison, *Sources and Documents Illustrating the American Revolution*, p. 119.

55. Quoted in Morison, *Sources and Documents Illustrating the American Revolution*, p. 121.

56. Quoted in Commager and Morris, *The Spirit of 'Seventy-Six*, p. 47.

57. Quoted in Robert A. Gross, *The Minutemen and Their World*, 6th ed. New York: Hill and Wang, 1977, p. 59.

58. Quoted in Commager and Morris, *The Spirit of 'Seventy-Six*, p. 61.

### Chapter 6: Fighting Begins

59. Quoted in Forbes, *Paul Revere and the World He Lived In*, p. 225.

60. Quoted in Forbes, *Paul Revere and the World He Lived In*, p. 238.

61. Quoted in Commager and Morris, *The Spirit of 'Seventy-Six*, p. 69.

62. Quoted in Middlekauff, *The Glorious Cause*, p. 270.

63. Smith, *A New Age Now Begins*, vol. 1, p. 481.

64. Quoted in Louis Birnbaum, *Red Dawn at Lexington*. Boston: Houghton Mifflin, 1986, pp. 91, 92.

65. Quoted in Wright, *Fabric of Freedom*, pp. 91, 92.

66. Quoted in Ketchum, *The World of George Washington*, p. 71.

67. Quoted in Ketchum, *The World of George Washington*, p. 72.

68. Quoted in Ketchum, *The World of George Washington*, p. 72.

69. Quoted in Morison, *The Oxford History of the American People*, vol. 1, p. 290.

70. Quoted in Commager and Morris, *The Spirit of 'Seventy-Six*, p. 150.

71. Quoted in Morison, *The Oxford History of the American People*, vol. 1, p. 290.

72. Quoted in Morris, *The American Revolution*, p. 54.

73. Quoted in Kallich and MacLeish, *The American Revolution Through British Eyes*, p. 79.

74. Quoted in Middlekauff, *The Glorious Cause*, p. 315.

75. Morison and Commager, *The Growth of the American Republic*, vol. 1, p. 187.

### Chapter 7: The Spirit of 'Seventy-Six

76. Thomas Paine, *Common Sense and Other Political Writings*. Edited by Nelson F. Adkins. New York: Liberal Arts Press (division of Bobbs-Merrill), 1953, p. 18.

77. Paine, *Common Sense*, p. 32.

78. Paine, *Common Sense*, p. 23.

79. Morgan, *The Birth of the Republic*, p. 76.

80. Quoted in Morison, *The Oxford History of the American People*, vol. 1, p. 292.

81. Quoted in Ketchum, *The World of George Washington*, p. 120.

82. Quoted in Morison, *The Oxford History of the American People*, vol. 1, p. 294.

83. Quoted in Morison, *The Oxford History of the American People*, vol. 1, p. 294.

84. Quoted in Commager and Morris, *The Spirit of 'Seventy-Six*, p. 320.

85. Quoted in Morison, *The Oxford History of the American People*, vol. 1, p. 296.

86. Morison, *The Oxford History of the American People*, vol. 1, p. 296.

87. Quoted in Richard B. Morris and the editors of Life, *The Making of a Nation*, vol. 2. New York: Time, Book Division, 1963, p. 28.

88. Paine, *Common Sense*, p. 55.

89. Quoted in Smith, *A New Age Now Begins*, vol. 1, p. 822.

### Chapter 8: War and Peace

90. Quoted in Commager and Morris, *The Spirit of 'Seventy-Six*, p. 581.

91. Quoted in Clark, *Benjamin Franklin*, p. 338.

92. Quoted in Morison, *Sources and Documents Illustrating the American Revolution*, p. 203.

93. Quoted in Commager and Morris, *The Spirit of 'Seventy-Six*, p. 649.

94. Smith, *A New Age Now Begins*, vol. 2, p. 1018.

95. Quoted in James Thomas Flexner, *Washington, The Indispensable Man*. 1969. Reprint, Boston: Little, Brown, 1975, p. 118.

96. Quoted in Flexner, *Washington*, p. 123.

97. Quoted in Smith, *A New Age Now Begins*, vol. 2, p. 1412.

98. Quoted in Commager and Morris, *The Spirit of 'Seventy-Six*, p. 1132.

99. Quoted in Commager and Morris, *The Spirit of 'Seventy-Six*, p. 1135.

100. Quoted in Jack P. Greene and J. R. Pole, eds., *The Blackwell Encyclopedia of the American Revolution*. Cambridge, MA: Blackwell, 1991, p. 728.

101. Quoted in Morison, *The Oxford History of the American People*, vol. 1, p. 342.

102. Quoted in Rutman, *The Morning of America*, p. 185.

103. Quoted in Clark, *Benjamin Franklin*, p. 384.

### Chapter 9: "A New Scene Opens"

104. Quoted in Commager and Morris, *The Spirit of 'Seventy-Six*, pp. 1288, 1289.

105. Rutman, *The Morning of America*, pp. 196–97.

106. Quoted in Morison, *Sources and Documents Illustrating the American Revolution*, p. 216.

107. Quoted in Merrill Jensen, ed., *The Documentary History of the Ratification of the Constitu-tion*, vol. 1, *Constitutional Documents and Records, 1776–1787*. Madison: State Historical Society of Wisconsin, 1976, p. 184.

108. Quoted in Jensen, *The Documentary History of the Ratification of the Constitution*, vol. 1, p. 187.

109. Quoted in Gaillard Hunt, ed., *The Writings of James Madison*, vol. 2, *1783–1787*. New York: G. P. Putnam's Sons, 1901, p. 361.

110. Quoted in Flexner, *Washington, The Indispensable Man*, p. 203.

111. Quoted in Niles, *Chronicles of the American Revolution*, p. 338.

112. Quoted in Wright, *Fabric of Freedom*, p. 165.

113. Bailyn, *Faces of the Revolution*, p. 228.

114. Rutman, *The Morning of America*, p. 211.

115. Quoted in Catherine Drinker Bowen, *Miracle at Philadelphia*. 1966. Reprint, New York: Book-of-the-Month Club, 1986, p. 130.

116. Quoted in Padover, *The World of the Founding Fathers*, p. 171.

117. Quoted in Flexner, *Washington, The Indispensable Man*, p. 209.

118. Quoted in Richard B. Morris, *The Framing of the Federal Constitution*. Washington, DC: National Park Service, U.S. Department of the Interior, 1986, p. 78.

### Epilogue: Legacy of Hope

119. Paul Wilstach, ed., *Correspondence of John Adams and Thomas Jefferson (1812-1826)*. Indianapolis: Bobbs-Merrill, 1925, p. 116.

120. Roy P. Basler, ed., *Abraham Lincoln, Speeches and Writings 1859–1865*. New York: Library of America, 1984, p. 213.

# For Further Reading

Leonard W. Cowie, *The Pilgrim Fathers*. New York: G. P. Putnam's Sons, 1972. Traces the early years of the Pilgrims in England and Holland. Re-creates the dangerous voyage of the *Mayflower* and the subsequent struggle of the tiny Plymouth colony to survive. Describes everyday life, the settlers' relations with the Indians, and the contributions of their leaders—the Pilgrim fathers. Interesting illustrations throughout.

Trevor Nevitt Dupuy, *The Military History of Revolutionary Land Battles*. New York: Franklin Watts, 1970. The author, a retired U.S. Army colonel, describes land battles from Lexington and Concord to the final battle at Yorktown. Illustrated with detailed maps of each battle.

Doris Faber and Harold Faber, *The Birth of a Nation*. New York: Charles Scribner's Sons, 1989. Describes the new nation's early years from Washington's election as the first president to his farewell address at the end of his second term. An excellent, readable overview of how the Constitution was put into practice.

Howard Fast, *April Morning*. 1961. Reprint (paperback), New York: Bantam, 1975. A historical novel that focuses on one day in the life of fifteen-year-old Adam Cooper. When the Redcoats march into Lexington on April 19, 1775, Adam is caught up in the excitement. But when his father is killed, he begins to understand the horrors of war. A fast-paced, gripping story about the day a boy and his country came of age.

Esther Forbes, *Johnny Tremain*. 1943. Reprint (paperback), Boston: Houghton Mifflin, 1960. A classic historical novel about an apprentice in Boston in 1774. After a crippling injury to his hand prevents him from continuing his apprenticeship, young Johnny Tremain becomes an express rider for the Committee of Safety, meeting such people as Paul Revere and John Hancock. He even disguises himself as a British soldier to find his friend Rab, wounded at Lexington. An absorbing story that captures the drama of the stirring days that preceded the Declaration of Independence.

Ann Rinaldi, *The Fifth of March, A Story of the Boston Massacre*. San Diego, CA: Harcourt Brace, 1993. Fourteen-year-old Rachel Marsh is an indentured servant in the Boston household of John and Abigail Adams at the time of the Boston Massacre. In this exciting story, Rachel is caught up in the intrigues and dangers of those pre-Revolution days in Boston.

Carolyn Kott Washburne, *A Multicultural Portrait of Colonial Life*. New York: Marshall Cavendish, 1994. An excellent work that describes colonial history from the point of view of minorities and women. Numerous maps, photos, and sidebars embellish this well-designed, understandable book.

# Works Consulted

Mortimer J. Adler, editor in chief, *The Annals of America*. Vol. 1, *1493–1754, Discovering a New World*. Chicago: Encyclopaedia Britannica, 1968. This first of eighteen volumes contains letters, tracts, documents, poems, and first-person accounts of historical events. The entries address a variety of subjects which range from the well-known "Mayflower Compact" to the lesser known "Connecticut Blue Laws."

Bernard Bailyn, *Faces of the Revolution*. New York: Knopf, 1990. Twelve essays that examine the background and legacy of the American Revolution, as well as the lives of some important—and not so important—people of the revolutionary era.

———, *The Ideological Origins of the American Revolution*. Cambridge, MA: The Belknap Press of Harvard University Press, 1967. A fascinating study of the assumptions, beliefs, and ideas that led to the American Revolution as expressed in the pamphlets and other writings of the time.

———, *Pamphlets of the American Revolution, 1750–1776*. Cambridge, MA: The Belknap Press of Harvard University Press, 1965. Collection of pamphlets written by revolutionaries from the early days until the Declaration of Independence.

Roy P. Basler, ed., *Abraham Lincoln, Speeches and Writings 1859–1865*. New York: Library of America, 1984. A collection of Lincoln's speeches, letters and miscellaneous writings, presidential messages and proclamations.

Louis Birnbaum, *Red Dawn at Lexington*. Boston: Houghton Mifflin, 1986. Dramatic, exciting in-depth account of the first military clash between Britain and the colonists.

Michael Blow, ed., *The American Heritage History of the Thirteen Colonies*. American Heritage, 1967. Explanatory text coupled with "In Their Own Words" documents and letters of the early settlers. Contains many interesting photographs.

Paul F. Boller Jr. and Ronald Story, eds., *A More Perfect Union, Documents in U.S. History*. Volume I, *To 1877*. Boston: Houghton Mifflin, 1984. Contains the familiar, as well as the less familiar, documents that illustrate America's political and social history to 1877.

Catherine Drinker Bowen, *John Adams and the American Revolution*. 1949. Reprint, Boston: Little, Brown, 1950. A "fictionalized biography," well researched and historically accurate. This very readable book brings John Adams and his contemporaries to life.

———, *Miracle at Philadelphia*. 1966. Reprint, New York: Book-of-the-Month Club, 1986. A descriptive, suspenseful narrative about the Constitutional Convention. Begins with the arrival of the delegates in Philadelphia and ends with the ratification of the Constitution.

Sculley Bradley, Richmond Croom Beatty, E. Hudson Long, and George Perkins, eds., *The American Tradition in Literature.* Vol. 1, 4th ed. 1956. Reprint, New York: Grosset & Dunlap, 1974. Anthology of American literature beginning with William Bradford of the Plymouth colony and ending with nineteenth-century poet Walt Whitman.

L. H. Butterfield, ed., *Diary and Autobiography of John Adams.* Vol. 2. Cambridge, MA: The Belknap Press of Harvard University Press, 1961. Adams's diary entries and observations for the years 1771 to 1781.

Ronald W. Clark, *Benjamin Franklin: A Biography.* New York: Random House, 1983. A balanced biography that shows Franklin's flaws as well as his genius.

Henry Steele Commager and Richard B. Morris, eds., *The Spirit of 'Seventy-Six, The Story of the American Revolution as Told by Participants.* 1958. Reprint, New York: Harper & Row, 1967. An outstanding source of British and colonial American letters, speeches, documents, newspaper accounts, broadsides, and pamphlets from 1776 through the ratification of the Constitution.

Hector St. John de Crèvecoeur, *Letters from an American Farmer.* Reprint, London: J. M. Dent & Sons, 1951. An often idealized account of life in colonial America, the author's adopted land. This classic work, praising democracy, is still enjoyable reading.

James Thomas Flexner, *Washington, The Indispensable Man.* 1969. Reprint, Boston: Little, Brown, 1974. A critically acclaimed classic biography of the first president of the United States of America.

Esther Forbes, *Paul Revere and the World He Lived In.* 1942. Reprint, New York: Book-of-the-Month Club, 1983. A highly readable, vivid account that draws the reader into the exciting world of yesteryear, a world of intrigue and danger—the world of Paul Revere.

Larry R. Gerlach, ed., *Legacies of the American Revolution.* Logan: Utah State University, 1978. Scholarly essays and lectures of ten prominent historians devoted to an assessment of America's revolutionary heritage in observation of the nation's two hundredth anniversary.

Jack P. Greene and J. R. Pole, eds., *The Blackwell Encyclopedia of the American Revolution.* Cambridge, MA: Blackwell, 1991. A scholarly, readable compilation of articles discussing all facets of the Revolution. Contains minibiographies of all British and American participants in the Revolution and a chronological table of political and legal events, military campaigns, and social, cultural, economic, scientific, and religious developments from 1688 to 1791.

Robert A. Gross, *The Minutemen and Their World.* 6th ed. New York: Hill and Wang, 1977. A detailed, well-written, well-researched history of eighteenth-century Concord, Massachusetts. Describes the impact of the Revolution on the daily lives of ordinary people in Concord.

Alexander Hamilton, James Madison, and John Jay, *The Federalist Papers.* New York: New American Library, 1961.

Contains eighty-five essays by three of the most original thinkers in American history, written to promote ratification of the Constitution.

David Hawke, ed., *U.S. Colonial History, Readings and Documents*. Indianapolis and New York: Bobbs-Merrill, 1966. Documents and readings beginning with Marco Polo's report on his travels and ending with James Madison's defense of the Constitution.

Gaillard Hunt, ed., *The Writings of James Madison*. Vol. 2, *1783–1787*. New York: G. P. Putnam's Sons, 1901. Madison's public papers and private correspondence.

Thomas Jefferson, *The Declaration of Independence: The Evolution of the Text as Shown in Facsimiles of Various Drafts by Its Author, Thomas Jefferson*. Edited by Julian P. Boyd. Princeton, NJ: Princeton University Press, 1945. Begins with Jefferson's original draft of the Declaration of Independence and includes various edits of the declaration by Jefferson and others, culminating in the final official document.

Merrill Jensen, ed., *The Documentary History of the Ratification of the Constitution*. Vol. 1, *Constitutional Documents and Records, 1776–1787*. Madison: State Historical Society of Wisconsin, 1976. A documentary history of the ratification of the Constitution with helpful introductory comments by the editor.

———, *The Founding of a Nation, A History of the American Revolution 1763–1776*. New York: Oxford University Press, 1968. A political history that stresses the deeds of men on both sides of the Atlantic that led to America's separation from England.

Martin Kallich and Andrew MacLeish, eds., *The American Revolution Through British Eyes*. New York: Harper & Row, 1962. A collection of documents that illustrate the reactions to the Revolution of a variety of Britons, including poets, politicians, merchants, and military officers. Shows the differences of opinion among the British regarding the future of the American colonies.

John F. Kennedy, *A Nation of Immigrants*. New York and Evanston: Harper & Row, 1964. An engrossing, fast-moving account of the important contribution of immigrants to American culture and progress.

Richard M. Ketchum, *The World of George Washington*. New York: American Heritage, 1974. A coffee-table book. Spare but accurate text with excellent photographs, maps, and sketches.

Peter B. Levy, ed., *100 Key Documents in American Democracy*. Westport, CT: Greenwood Press, 1994. Historical documents from 1609 colonial America through 1988.

Henry Wadsworth Longfellow, *The Complete Poetical Works of Henry Wadsworth Longfellow*. Boston: Houghton, Mifflin; Cambridge, MA: The Riverside Press, 1884. Collected poems of Longfellow with illustrations.

E.V. Lucas, ed., *William Cowper's Letters*. London: Oxford University Press, 1908. Selected letters of the poet William Cowper, with footnotes by the editor.

Frank N. Magill, ed., *Great Events from History* (American Series). Vol. 1. 1907. Reprint, Englewood Cliffs, NJ: Salem Press, 1975. Part of a three-volume series that covers U.S. history from Unknown to 1830. Offers a succinct summary of each event followed by a list of recommended sources for further information. This volume begins with "Arrival of the Indians, the First Americans," and ends with the "Passage of the Indian Removal Act in 1830."

Joseph Plumb Martin, *Private Yankee Doodle. Being a Narrative of Some of the Adventures, Dangers and Sufferings of a Revolutionary Soldier.* Edited by George F. Scheer. New York: New York Times and Arno Press, 1968. An eyewitness account of the American Revolution written with wit and irony.

Robert Middlekauff, *The Glorious Cause, The American Revolution, 1763–1789.* New York: Oxford University Press, 1982. Begins with the Treaty of Paris, which ended the French and Indian War, and details the growing conflict between America and England. Devotes special attention to military campaigns and strategies, with maps of major battles. Ends with Washington's election to the presidency.

Perry Miller and Thomas H. Johnson, eds., *The Puritans.* Vol. 2. 1938. Reprint, New York: Harper & Row, 1963. Selected Puritan writings that reflect the manners, customs, and scientific ideas of the time. Biographies and letters. Helpful editorial comments throughout.

Frank Moore, *Diary of the American Revolution.* New York: Charles T. Evans, 1863.

Selections from newspapers and original documents of the revolutionary era.

Edmund S. Morgan, *The Birth of the Republic, 1763–89,* 15th ed. Chicago: University of Chicago Press, 1969. Concise, clearly written, readable history of the American Revolution, beginning with the French and Indian War and ending with the ratification of the Constitution.

Samuel Eliot Morison, *The Oxford History of the American People.* Vol. 1. 1965. Reprint, New York: Penguin Books, 1972. In this volume, the Pulitzer Prize–winning historian presents a comprehensive history of the American people from the earliest Indian civilizations to the beginnings of George Washington's first administration. This very readable book is both scholarly and entertaining.

Samuel Eliot Morison, ed., *Sources and Documents Illustrating the American Revolution, 1764–1788 and the Formation of the Federal Constitution.* 2nd ed. Oxford: Oxford University Press, 1961. Includes important documents, debates, letters, and pamphlets, with extensive documentation devoted to the forming and ratification of the Constitution.

Samuel Eliot Morison and Henry Steele Commager, *The Growth of the American Republic.* Vol. 1. 5th ed. New York: Oxford University Press, 1962. Overview of American history from 1492 through Lincoln's assassination in 1865. Contains maps and illustrations.

Richard B. Morris, *The American Revolution, A Short History.* 1955. Reprint,

New York: Krieger, 1979. A short account of the revolutionary era. Begins with the French and Indian War and ends with the Treaty of Paris in 1783. Analyzes causes of the war. Half the book is devoted to a wide variety of historical documents and important speeches.

————, *The Framing of the Federal Constitution*. Washington, DC: National Park Service, U.S. Department of the Interior, 1986. Tells the story of the creation and ratification of the federal Constitution in simple, easy-to-read prose. Many interesting illustrations and photographs.

Richard B. Morris and the editors of Life, *The Making of a Nation*. Vol. 2. New York: Time, Book Division, 1963. Chronicle of events of the American Revolution in text and pictures.

Gary B. Nash and Julie Roy Jeffrey et al., eds., *The American People, Creating a Nation and a Society*. New York: Harper & Row, 1986. A college textbook that provides a comprehensive survey of American history from 1492 to 1985.

Hezekiah Niles, *Chronicles of the American Revolution*. Edited by Alden T. Vaughan. New York: Grosset & Dunlap, 1965. Collected documents, letters, debates, and speeches from the period of the Stamp Act to the Constitution. Editorial comments by Niles, who witnessed the Revolution.

Saul K. Padover, *Jefferson*. 1942. Reprint, New York: New American Library, 1970. Classic biography of Thomas Jefferson.

————, *The World of the Founding Fathers*. 1960. Reprint, Cranbury, NJ: Barnes, 1977. Speeches, writings, and letters of the founders, with clarifying editorial introductions to each one.

Thomas Paine, *Common Sense and Other Political Writings*. Edited by Nelson F. Adkins. New York: Liberal Arts Press (division of Bobbs-Merrill), 1953. Originally printed as pamphlets, *Common Sense* and *The Crisis* had an immeasurable impact on American history.

Kenneth Pearson and Patricia Connor, eds., *1776, The British Story of the American Revolution*. London: Times Newspapers, 1976. Prepared for the 1976 exhibition at the National Maritime Museum in the United Kingdom. Contains articles on the American Revolution by prominent historians along with photographs and illustrations.

Jack N. Rakove, *The Beginnings of National Politics, An Interpretive History of the Continental Congress*. New York: Knopf, 1979. Revolutionary politics and government from 1783 to 1789 with special emphasis on the Articles of Confederation and the movement toward a stronger national government.

Darrett B. Rutman, *The Morning of America, 1603–1789*. Boston: Houghton Mifflin, 1971. A detailed, illuminating study with emphasis on the colonial experience and how it culminated in the Revolution.

Page Smith, *A New Age Now Begins*, Vol. 1. New York: McGraw-Hill, 1976. An extensive narrative of the American Revolution in two volumes, written for the general reader. Volume 1 begins with the first colonial settlers and ends in 1776.

————, *A New Age Now Begins*. Vol. 2. New York: McGraw-Hill, 1976. Extends the narrative begun in volume 1 through the Paris peace treaty.

Paul Wilstach, ed., *Correspondence of John Adams and Thomas Jefferson (1812-1826)*. Indianapolis: Bobbs-Merrill, 1925. Letters between two Founding Fathers in the last years of their lives.

Ola Elizabeth Winslow, ed., *Harper's Literary Museum, Early American Writings*. New York: Harper & Brothers, 1927. A selection of early American writings, some thought provoking, some entertaining.

Esmond Wright, *Fabric of Freedom, 1763–1800*. 1961. Reprint, New York: Hill and Wang (division of Farrar, Straus and Giroux), 1964. History of the Revolution through 1800; focuses on the emergence of an American nationality and on that "fabrick of freedom": democracy.

Esmond Wright, ed., *The Fire of Liberty*. New York: St. Martin's Press, 1983. Documents and letters that present the American War of Independence through the eyes of the men and women, the statesmen, and the soldiers who fought it.

# Index

# Picture Credits

Cover photo by SCALA/Art Resource, NY

Dover Publications, 35, 37 (both), 38, 42, 43, 45, 46, 48, 51, 58, 59, 61, 76, 81, 88, 110

Library of Congress, 11 (top), 13, 14, 22, 26, 28, 29 (bottom), 30, 32, 47 (bottom), 52, 60, 63, 65, 68, 69, 70, 71, 73, 74, 75, 78, 79 (both), 80, 83 (both), 87, 89, 90, 91, 92 (both), 100, 104, 108, 111

National Archives, 67

North Wind Picture Archives, 11 (bottom), 23, 29 (top)

# About the Author

Bonnie L. Lukes is a freelance writer living in southern California. She graduated from California State University, Northridge, with a major in English literature.

She has published essays and stories in a wide variety of magazines and newspapers. Her book *How to Be a Reasonably Thin Teenage Girl* was chosen by the National Council of Books for Children as an Outstanding Science Trade Book.